Francesca Russo
Emanuele Santi

FEAR NO MORE

Voices of the Tunisian Revolution

Foreword by Eamonn Gearon

This book records stories and events, as witnessed by many people. Names of some of these people have been changed in order to protect their identities.

ISBN 979-87-860-1743-5

Front cover photo: © Saif Chaabane
Back cover photo: Francesca Russo
Copy Editors: Kaylen Camacho McCluskey, Evelyn Pali, Sally Ash
Amazon editions Editor: Gian Luca Zanotti
Book Coordinator and communications: Chara Tsitoura

TABLE OF CONTENTS

To the victims and martyrs of the Tunisian Revolution,
their families, and all the small and big heroes
who had the courage
to fight for their freedom and dignity
and set an unforgettable example
for the rest of the world.

To all those seeking freedom from oppression.

To our sons Edoardo and Raffaele,
who patiently sensed and shared our emotions,
often unaware, being a valuable source of distraction,
but also, our greatest concern during the darkest moments.
This is a legacy for them for their time in Tunisia
and a means to appreciate the value of freedom.

NOTE ON THE AUTHORS

Started as a blog to reach out to the world about the events occurring in Tunisia, this book-to-be turned into a lively collective work enriched with interviews from Tunisian activists, artists, journalists, families of the 'martyrs' of the revolution, as well as ordinary people. These are Tunisians and non-Tunisians from across the globe. From Tunisia to Europe, from Australia to the United States, even passing through Dubai, many contributed with ideas, input, reviews and more to this 'collective' book.

The main authors of the book are a young couple. She is a cultural anthropologist. He is an economist. Both have extensive experience and knowledge of North Africa. They moved to Tunisia in 2007, and left the country shortly after the first democratic election. They have spent over a decade living and traveling across Africa, Asia and America, pursuing their interest in developing countries and working for international organizations. Africa is the continent where they belong and where they experienced the most defining moments of their lives.

The authors would like to thank all those people who took part in the realization of this book, namely Hakim Ben Hammouda, Simone Santi, Najib Chouaibi, Silvia Costantini, Mourad Ben Cheikh, Mohamed Malouche, Francesca Bellino, Ahmed Hafiene, Carlo Svaluto Moreolo, Saoussen Ben Romdhane, Jaouher Dalhoumi, Monique Vassart, Lori Broglio Severens, Claudio Piazzi, Massimo Bevacqua and Chara Tsitoura.

FOREWORD

A dramatic, tightly-woven and fast-moving book, *Fear No More* tells the story of the truly momentous events that occurred across Tunisia in December 2010 and January 2011, from the self-immolation and death of Mohammad Bouazizi, a fruit vendor in a nondescript town that tourists have no need to visit, to the ouster and flight of one of the most venal and autocratic rulers to be found anywhere in the Greater Middle East – a region where there is fierce competition for such a title.

When I was approached to write this foreword, I made no promises to the authors – Francesca Russo and Emanuele Santi – beyond agreeing to read the manuscript of *Fear No More* and letting them know what I thought. Time is precious, and who ever has enough of it to say yes to all of the things we would like to do? How many emails remain unwritten, holidays untaken, books left unread?

When I received the manuscript, I was extremely busy. I was about to start teaching a new postgraduate course on North Africa from independence to the so-called 'Arab Spring,' I was staring at a teetering pile of books waiting to be reviewed, there were appearances scheduled on panels of the great and the good, discussions about Tunisia and the rest of North Africa two years on from the start of the Arab uprisings. And there was trouble in Mali: a long-standing Tuareg rebellion and the rise of al-Qaeda and other makers of mayhem in a remote and usually ignored part of the Sahara.

But, having agreed to read *Fear No More*, I printed out the manuscript and sat down one morning, planning to read for just half hour before getting on with my day, returning to read a little more of this book when I could find the time. I started reading and did not stop until I reached the last line on the final page. Breakfast time had long since passed, but I was not hungry; my pot of tea was two-hours empty, but I was not thirsty. It is an all too rare joy to start reading a book and to find oneself so immersed, so enthralled that one keeps reading until the end in a single sitting. *Fear No More* is one such book.

A country best known as a tourist destination on the southern shores of the Mediterranean, just an hour's flight from Rome, and only three from London, Tunisia was perhaps thought by many as an unlikely setting for a popular revolution that would set the region alight. Politically speaking, Tunisia is not so much a trendsetter as a backwater, better known for beaches than barricades. But away from the tourist resorts, the country had long been a repressive police state, corrupt and in many ways rotten to the core. Tunisians did not make jokes about their president, at least not in public.

This and other often-overlooked aspects of Tunisia's recent history are brought into sharp focus in *Fear No More*. Overall, the story told is especially powerful for the authors' wise decision to use the words and thoughts of Tunisians in addition to their own observations. Natives and foreigners will always see things in different ways, and bringing both voices together here lends the whole text additional strength.

Where an expatriate might not understand some subtlety of language or a deep cultural reference, Francesca and Emanuele are happy to let the Tunisians – bloggers, activists, teachers, lawyers, housewives and students – speak for themselves: when their view as outsiders offers a distinct view, not otherwise available to a local, they come to the fore, as guides to all outsiders keen to understand something more about what happened in Tunisia at the start of 2011.

I love Tunisia, and I am grateful for all the memories and friends I have made there over the years: students, teachers, booksellers, barmen, waiters in cafés, landlords, my cleaner and even my smiling dentist! When I recall the fruit and vegetable sellers who plied their trade in the Tunis neighborhood I once called home, it is their faces that most quickly remind me of Mohammad Bouazizi and the mass of ordinary Tunisians. Hardworking men and women endured more than just the quotidian struggles of life, being forced to deal with these as well as a system that was stacked against them. Under Ben Ali, the system worked on connections not talent; a willingness to work hard counted little next to the man with *wasta*, influence.

At the time of writing, Tunisia's journey towards better times is somewhat smoother than that of others in the region, although with moments of turmoil ahead. After decades of corruption and political cronyism, the road to recovery and an even brighter future will not be straight or swift, there will be some dark days, but Tunisians are up to the challenge. *Fear No More*: is an entirely apt title for what took place in Tunisia in 2011, and it is a sentiment that continues to reverberate as the country looks forwards, and which other countries look to with a degree of envy.

Nearly seven million tourists visited Tunisia in 2010. This figure was lower in 2011, as the country went through its revolution: the numbers are sure to rise again, because Tunisia is too good to miss. Now, when tourists go to explore Tunisia – or return to revisit old haunts – they can count themselves lucky to have in *Fear No More* as a guidebook that offers them something far more important than advice about where to sleep or dine in style.

Eamonn Gearon
Professor of North African Studies at Johns Hopkins University (SAIS)

INTRODUCTION

I am the place where something has occurred.

Claude Lévi Strauss

It's the eve of a major anti-government protest on January 14th 2011, a date that will be forever engraved in the history of Tunisia and beyond. There's a strange feeling in the hours preceding great events that remains undefined and uncertain. It's a premonition comprised of excitement, expectations and fears. We are glued to the keyboard, connected to our friends through the internet. We exchange news, articles and real time reports from activists, protesters turned journalists, and even doctors reporting on citizens attacked by the police. The news is spreading quickly by word of mouth. Tunisians living abroad seem to be right around the corner from us, posting uncensored information on the web. News is being reported live, giving us the illusion of actually walking along Avenue Bourguiba, one of the central streets of Tunis, where major events take place. The invitations to join demonstrations are overwhelming, and so is the new space open to videos and posts that were previously censored.

It's impossible to focus on anything else. The rapidity with which the information travels is frantic. Newspapers seem to launch news hesitantly and with delay, reporting actions we already know about through social media. Even so, we can't help following them. We need to keep up with the latest events. The first thing we notice is the difference between two versions of reality that seem to be growing apart. On one hand, there are Facebook, Twitter and YouTube, which have just resumed working in Tunisia after years of censorship and quickly become a true "agora" of discontent. On the other, there are the famous international newspapers, reporting the same old news on the 'Tunisian situation', often labeling the events a mere 'Bread Riot'[1], and overlooking their deeply political nature of the protest, going beyond economic want. This is somewhat exemplified by one of the most popular slogans used by protesters: 'Bread and water, no to Ben Ali'.

Sharing news picks up an unprecedented pace among Tunisians. We try to do the same, keeping all our friends, near and far, informed about what is happening. We want the world to know. It is our modest contribution to the ongoing event – through simple gestures, we link to a wider movement with ample ramifications in Tunisia and beyond. Our family blog and Facebook walls are dominated by posts recalling demonstrations, shootings, screams, the clatter of helicopters, but the sense of solidarity and perseverance persists. There we are, trying to explain to our two small kids just what is happening, but the words are often missing.

The idea of writing a book solidifies during our brief evacuation to Italy, when we feel the need to challenge the often simplistic views of the Tunisian Revolution. We feel that similarly to November 9th 1989, the date marking the fall of the Berlin Wall,

[1] Ciezadlo, A, Let Them Eat Bread, How Food Subsidies Prevent (and Provoke) Revolutions in the Middle East, Foreign Affairs, March 23, 2011.

January 14th 2011 will be a landmark in the history of the Middle East and North Africa and beyond. The success of the Tunisian Revolution marks the fall of the wall of fear felt by all Tunisians for more than 20 years under an authoritarian regime, acting as a powerful inspiration to many other countries. It is the end of the hegemony of a single party that prevailed by deceitfully promising stability and prosperity, at the expense of limited freedom. It also prompted a shift in the political positions of most western countries, who felt that Arab populations were not able to choose an adequate leader capable of confronting Islamic fundamentalism.

The fall of the Berlin Wall weakened all Communist regimes. The fall of the 'Tunis Wall of Fear', as experienced by many people we interviewed, revealed a discrepancy between the totalitarian regimes in the region – throwing the relationship between citizens and authorities into question beyond geographical, political and cultural borders. Tunisians prevailed by overcoming their fear of the ruling structure of power, which fueled hope of a promising future for the rest of the Arab world and beyond. It proved that the desire for freedom and dignity is a universal aspiration, irrespective of the will of the 'great powers'. These are the principles of this book, based on the events of 30 days that made freedom available to all Tunisians.

Our aim is to give a different perspective on the facts experienced by the Tunisians who took part in the demonstrations, and by people like us who felt in many ways part of this movement, more virtually than physically - yet still present, with our eyes and ears, as well as our voices. This book records a chronological chain of events. It describes the sequence and the crescendo of the events that took place from the spark ignited on December

17th 2010, when a street seller sacrificed himself to reclaim his dignity. This event triggered an unexpected change not only in the country but also in the entire region. Only a few months before, the same act of desperation by a young boy in Monastir had sparked no such reaction among the people. At that time, lawyers and students were not ready to support the idea of a unique revolution.

Fear No More recounts how every single character in this book managed to overcome his or her fear and had the courage to re-establish the karama, or dignity, previously suppressed by violence and punishment. It is the collection of personal experiences of the authors, enriched by hundreds of letters and messages posted on Facebook, which became the most important source of information in Tunisia, and where 2 of 10 million Tunisians had an account. Facebook became a virtual 'town square' where people could express their differing opinions, organize demonstrations through coded messages, and be informed of impending dangers. It also enabled Tunisians living abroad – and many more from other nations – to unite and become part of a global movement on the web.

Not only this book is the result of interviews and long chats with the revolution's major movers and shakers, but also ordinary people, who played their own modest yet important roles. Among them were artists, activists, students, bloggers, and the relatives of the 'martyrs' – men and women killed during the events – whose lives have been made eternal through local beliefs. We shared our experiences with our Tunisian and Italian friends, but especially with our children. During the period when we were prisoners in our home, just a few hundred meters away from the presidential palace in Carthage where some of the shooting and street fighting took place, our sons gave us moments of distraction and happiness, and helped maintain a sense of reality. How do you explain to a five and three-year-old why supermarkets are being robbed, doors barred, shootings becoming more and more frequent, and barricades blocking the streets?

Fear No More is a tribute to a population who succeeded in leading a revolution while still remembering its guests, like us, even in the most difficult moments.

It is also a salute to the victims and their families, who graciously opened up and shared their stories with us, involving us in a movement without borders, giving us the chance to understand their feelings and share one of the most fascinating chapters in the history of North Africa.

BEN ALI AND HIS 23-YEAR RULE

He who plants thorns shall not expect to gather roses.

Arab proverb

It is hard to understand the Tunisian revolution without taking into account the two decades marked by the regime of Ben Ali.

An ambitious career soldier raised to the rank of prime minister, Ben Ali took over the presidency of Tunisia through a so-called 'medical *coup d'état*' on November 7th 1987, when he convinced the doctors of the former President Bourguiba (first leader of independence and symbol of resistance against the French) to pronounce their patient mentally incapable of fulfilling his role[2]. The coup was supported by various foreign governments, such as Italy and its secret service, as was revealed many years later by Fulvio Martini[3], head of the Italian intelligence and security services under the government of Bettino Craxi.[4] The coup took place when the country was about

---

[2] Nicolas Beau, Jean-Pierre Tuquoi et Gilles Perrault, Notre ami Ben Ali. L'envers du miracle tunisien, éd. La Découverte, Paris, 2002.

[3] Carlo Chianura, "L'Italia dietro il golpe in Tunisia", La Repubblica, 10 October 1999.

[4] Bettino Craxi was head of the Italian Socialist Party from 1976 to 1993, the Prime Minister of Italy from 1983 to 1987. Accused in the 90s for corruption charges and often considered as the symbol of Italy's political corruption, Craxi escaped the Italian justice, by fleeing to Hammamet in Tunisia in 1994,

to experience an economic collapse and vulnerable to a military attack from Algeria and terrorist attacks from North Africa. Ben Ali decided at that time to create a 'restrained' democracy, resembling more of an authoritarian regime, in order to more easily counter such attacks. This 'security' seduced the population by persuading them that limiting political and individual freedom, and often sacrificing human rights, was a worthwhile price to pay in the fight against extremism[5].

After September 11th (9/11), Tunisia came to be seen as a symbol of the fight against terrorism. In April 2003, one year after the explosion of a bomb in a synagogue in Djerba that resulted in 17 victims, a strict anti-terrorist law was approved[6]. This jeopardized human rights by giving the authorities the power to arrest whoever was seen to be a threat to national security. So the witch hunts began.

Jihed Aounie was a 20-year-old boy who lived in a village near Sidi Bouzid, in the heart of Tunisia. In 2007, he was jailed for eight years after being found guilty of converting to the Shiite doctrine. The prosecutors accused him of being influenced by underground Islamic TV channels and forbidden books. As the lawyer responsible for his defense, Khaled Ouayniya, told us, the man was illiterate. His house had no electricity, and his family

---

and remained a fugitive there, protected by Ben Ali's government, until his death in 2000.

[5] Soumaya Gannoushi, Exposing the real Tunisia, The Guardian, 4 April 2011.

[6] Amnesty International, Le projet de loi " antiterroriste " porte un nouveau coup aux droits humains, 30 September 2003.

didn't even own a television. 'Nevertheless, this information wasn't enough to free the boy.' He was used as a scapegoat, forced to serve his sentence as a warning to the rest of the population. Khaled is one of many small heroes who did their best to counter the authoritarian regime of Ben Ali. He helped people like Jihed – and paid the price for it. Every now and then police would pay him a visit, or park outside his small office in Sidi Bouzid, harassing him and turning his potential clients and visitors away.

Ben Ali placed huge importance on the media, following the example of his predecessor, Bourguiba. He had full control of the press and radio, which were forced to project an image of a highly competent, successful and progressive leader. Pictures and interviews of Ben Ali were very often on the front page of newspapers and on public news channels, such as TV 7 and Channel 21, where his initiatives, along with his promises and achievements, were the lead stories. The situation improved slightly when new radio stations and independent TV channels became more and more available to Tunisians through satellite TV, but the principle was always the same – there was no place for opposing opinions. Opposition to the regime was not tolerated, and promptly dealt with by the government.

This was the case of Zouhair Yahyahoui, nicknamed 'Ettounsi' (The Tunisian). He was jailed for two years for creating a website dedicated to satirical opposition, which he called *Tunezine*[7] (a punning reference to Zine, the President's first name). He was subjected to torture and initiated three hunger

---

[7] www.tunezine.com

strikes, which drew the attention of the international media. After the third round of torture, Zouhair revealed the access code to his website, which was quickly shut down by the authorities. Once freed, he spent his days in and out of hospital, and died only a few months later of a heart attack.

International press such as *Le Monde, Liberation* and *Le Figaro,* that attempted to expose government corruption, human rights' abuses and the country's democratic deficit, were heavily censored.

According to Reporters Without Borders, journalists and human rights' activists were the targets of bureaucratic harassment, police aggression and intelligence surveillance. The government had direct control over news and information. The French newspaper *Le Monde,* considered the most influential paper amongst French and Tunisian intellectuals, hadn't been distributed since 2009, when it had mocked Ben Ali's overwhelming yet dubious re-election results (89.62% of votes).

Restraining measures were launched against the opposition. Non-governmental organizations, such as the Tunisian League for Human Rights, the Tunisian Bar Association and the Tunisian main trade union (UGTT), scarcely found wiggle-room in the press, especially when commenting on sensitive matters. The National Union of Tunisian Journalists had been under constant attack since publishing reports about restrictions on freedom of expression and media control[8].

'National newspapers adopted self-censorship measures in order to survive,' Omar S'Habou, director of *Le Maghreb* maga-

---

[8] Freedom House, "Tunisia" Freedom in the World 2010 https://freedomhouse.org/report/freedom-world/2010/tunisia

zine, wrote after the revolution enabled him to speak out. 'Ben Ali and his 23 year dictatorship have been a nightmare. As director of an independent and political magazine, I knew the hidden truths only too well. But rules were dictated by Ben Ali and his clan; I was powerless to report on the state of repression we were living in'[9].

Until just a few days before the Tunisian Revolution, internet users were used to the message *Error 404* appearing on computer screens when they tried to access certain websites. *YouTube* access was denied as it featured a number of anti-regime videos. *Al Jazeera* and *Al Arabiya* websites were also often censored. Other local sites run by activists, such as *Tunisinews, aafaq.org* and *nawaat.org,* were never accessible in Tunisia, although followed by many Tunisians abroad. In everyone's mind and in private conversations, censorship was represented by *Error 404,* which became known to activists as *Ammar 404* – an ironic codename representing the regime.

However, restrictions on human rights and information were tolerated overall by many people belonging to the Tunisian bourgeoisie. They were more inclined to consider these as the price to pay to live in a secure and wealthy environment, in what many defined as 'an island of stability' praised by the country's western allies. This conformism was often coupled with a sense of fatalism. 'A population whose dignity has been violated for such a long time may be persuaded that social and political dif-

[9] Dégage, La Révolution Tunisienne, Livre-Temoignage, Éditions du Layeur, Tunis, 2011.

ferences are God-willed,'[10] wrote Tahar Ben Jelloun, a Moroccan writer.

Tunisia was also different from its neighboring countries, such as Algeria and Libya, because it promoted foreign investments, resulting in bilateral negotiations and special partnerships with countries like France and Italy. The country was capable of attracting famous multinational companies such as British Gas, Total, Microsoft, Eni, Sanofi-Aventis, Nestlé, and Ansaldo. Despite the relatively small size of its market, Tunisia offered a safe haven in terms of security and a rather attractive investment climate, including a generous offshore regime used by many companies to avoid taxes back home.

Many employers took advantage of these conditions,' we were told by Aldo Gervasoni, a young entrepreneur who, attracted by the low cost of metal and electricity and favorable tax regime, took over a foundry with 140 employees. 'Many employers, especially in the textile sector, keep their employees under training contracts for about four years, which is the limit allowed, and then they pass them on to other companies offering the same conditions. And all this,' he told us with regret, 'normally happens under the eyes of powerless unions that are controlled by the government.'

Tunisia was also a popular holiday destination, particularly among Europeans who were often drawn to the 'all-inclusive' formula of four- and five-star hotels but rarely rubbed shoulders with the local population. The reality of the country was far from

---

[10] Ben Jelloun, La Rivoluzione dei Gelsomini, Il risveglio della dignità araba, Bompiani, Milan, 2011.

the glamorous image tourists used to see. Youth unemployment was one of the highest in the world, and the gap between the rich coastal cities and poor hinterlands where people lived in misery was and remains huge. Furthermore, corruption was widespread. The most lucrative businesses were in the hands of a very few people, and the only way to succeed was to know somebody, a 'godfather,' or a member of the president's family, who could guarantee protection.

Leila Trabelsi, Ben Ali's highly controversial second wife, became the center of an unprecedented economic and political power structure. Imed, her illegitimate son, became mayor of La Goulette and owner of the Bricorama, a do-it-yourself department store[11]. Nesrine, Leila's daughter, married Mohamed Sakher El Materi, an ambitious businessman, who quickly built an empire made of lucrative businesses, ranging from car dealerships and banks to telecommunication companies, and rose up to become a potential successor to Ben Ali[12]. Their palace in Hammamet, enriched with antiques, Roman columns and paintings, also boasted a sculpture of a lion's head, with water coming out of its mouth to fill a swimming pool. All this came to light by way of an American ambassador's reports, published by *WikiLeaks*, which described

---

[11] Maghreb Confidential: Imed Trabelsi Shakes up Bricorama, 935, 22 July 2010.

[12] Florence Beaugé, « Le parcours fulgurant de Sakhr El-Materi, gendre du président tunisien Ben Ali », Le Monde, 24 octobre 2009 http://www.lemonde.fr/afrique/article/2009/10/24/le-parcours-fulgurant-de-sakhr-el-materi-gendre-du-president-tunisien-ben-ali_1258326_3212.html

the various excesses and lavish behavior of El Materi, including his unusual pet – a tiger that would eat four chickens a day.

'The luxury they live in explains why many Tunisians hate El Materi, Nesrine and the rest of Ben Ali's family. This overindulgence is becoming unacceptable,' reported the US ambassador in one of the cables[13].

The economic empire of the Trabelsi family also included Belhassen, Leila's brother. Married to the daughter of Hédi Djilani, president of Tunisia's main business federation and key party executive of RCD (*Rassemblement Constitutionnel Democratique*, Tunisian ruling party under Ben Ali), Belhassen owned an airline, two radio stations, car dealerships, real estate agencies and luxury hotels. He also became owner of the Bank of Tunisia, thus consolidating the *de facto* monopoly of the Trabelsi family, especially in the country's banking system[14].

And the family became even richer, partially because of land speculation, when the value of land increased with the tourism boom. The government would sell land to Ben Ali's family members, who would then resell them at a much higher price. Leila Trabelsi bought a piece of land intended for a private school but sold it on again at an elevated price[15]. The confiscation commission set up by the new government after Ben Ali's fall estimated

---

[13] Troubled Tunisia: what should we do. (https://wikileaks.org/plusd/cables/09TUNIS492_a.html) www.wikileaks.org. Document date 17/07/2009, document released the 07/12/2010.

[14] Julie Calleeuw, « Tunisie : les Trabelsi, une « quasi-mafia » », RTBF, 14 January 2011.

[15] Philippe Douroux, La corruption de la famille Ben Ali vue par l'ambassade des Etats Unis, Au but de compte, Le Monde blog, 15 January 2011.

that the total value of the extended family assets combined was approximately 13 billion dollars, or more than a quarter of the Tunisian economy[16]. Corruption spread among members of Ben Ali's party, the RCD) and spilled over to the police. It was a corrupt system, based on both large and small favors. Despite this, many Tunisians supported Ben Ali until the end, often repeating that he was 'a good man surrounded by bad people'. The increase of corrupt practices also had a significant impact on the country's slowing growth performance, by leading investors to be more and more reluctant to take risks[17].

---

[16] According to a World Bank study In the aftermath of the Tunisian revolution, the new government order the confiscation of Ben Ali and his extended family assets by means of a decree (Décret-loi n° 2011-13). This operation, involved 114 individuals, including Ben Ali himself, his relatives and his in-laws. The seized assets included: 550 properties, 48 boats and yachts, 40 stock portfolios, 367 bank accounts, and approximately 400 enterprises (not all of which operate in Tunisia. Rijkers, B.,Freund, C., Nucifora, A., All in the family: the state capture in Tunisia, World Bank, 2014.

[17] Hakim Ben Hammouda, Tunisie: Economie Politique d'une Revolution, de Boeck, 2012.

PRELUDE TO THE REVOLUTION

*If a man will only realize that it is unmanly to obey rules that are
unjust, no man's tyranny will enslave him.*

Mahatma Gandhi

It is difficult to establish the precise day when the Tunisian Revolution began. Even though December 17th marks the historic date, the country had already been on the brink of revolution for quite a few years. The regime had faced its first big challenge at the beginning of 2008. This event, which involved the Gafsa mining region in the southeastern part of the country, signified the beginning of a slow process that led to the events in December 2010 and January 2011.

Gafsa was one of the country's richest areas because of its phosphate mines, but was also amongst the poorest in terms of living conditions. Tunisia is one of the world's biggest producers of phosphate[18], and finding a job in the mines is the only opportunity people have to earn a living given the distance from the main tourist and industrial areas. In past decades, the prices of phosphate had skyrocketed thanks to increased demand from China and India, which led to an upgrade of plants, coupled with a downsizing of the number of employees needed to work in the mines. The mining area was monopolized by the state

---

[18] Zapata, F., Roy, R. N., (ed.), Use of Phosphate Rocks for Sustainable Agriculture, FAO, Rome, 2004.

owned phosphate company, CPG (Compagnie de Phosphate de Gafsa). CPG had not recruited workers for years, and by 2008, the unemployment rate in the area reached 36%. The protest started on January 5th that same year, following the announcement of the results of a hiring contest. Out of thousands of participants, only 380 candidates had been selected, and without a transparent selection process. The following day, a group of protesters blocked the railway connecting the mines to the main plant. More protests were sparked in Redeyef, a city of 40,000 inhabitants, where rioters attacked symbols of Ben Ali's power and his authority, including CPG. Demonstrations and strikes were organized by workers and the unemployed to denounce corruption, poor working conditions and unfair recruitment by CPG[19].

The protest was described by Italian journalist Gabriele Del Grande, one of the few who ventured to the region and covered the event at the time.

'The chain of events can be seen as general proof of the recent past. Young unemployed men rebelled against the system and occupied the Secretariat of Regional Miners (UGTT) which was accused of being involved in the scandal. They were soon joined by 11 widows, who asked CPG to fulfill payment of the quota allotted to the children of those men who died at work. Meanwhile, in Tunis a national committee was created in support to the mines. A day of solidarity was held in Tunis, with the partic-

---

[19] Del Grande Gabriele, The dictatorship south of Lampedusa, 2 November 2008 in http://fortresseurope.blogspot.com/2006/01/tunisia-la-dittatura-sud-di-lampedusa.html

ipation of trade unionists from Redeyef. On their return home, on April 7th, the trade unionists were all arrested, together with dozens of activists. Among them was Adnan Hajji, the secretary of the Union of Teachers in Redeyef. On the same day, teachers in the whole city suspended lessons and called for a general strike, which lasted for three days. On April 9th, around 30 women descended on the streets, asking to have their husbands freed from prison. Many other citizens joined them in their appeal. The following day, the trade unionists were finally released. On their arrival into the city, a crowd of 20,000 people welcomed their new leader, Adnan Hajji. Meanwhile, initiatives of solidarity organized by Tunisian expats also spread in France, especially in Nantes, where a large community of Tunisians from Redeyef lives.'

The protests in the mining region did not cease. On May 6th 2008, Hicham Ben Jeddou died, after having received a fatal electrical shock while a group of young unemployed protestors occupied the generator of Tabeddit. Witnesses accused police of having turned on the electricity knowing that he was alongside the wires. It was the beginning of an unmatched wave of repression.

Reinforcements were sent from Tunis to the mining area. Police checked all the accesses to Redeyef, and plainclothes agents monitored the protest's leading figures. On June 6th, police opened fire on a demonstration. One man, Hafnaoui Maghzaoui, was killed, and 27 people were injured. One of the victims, Abdelkhaleq Aamidi, died three months later on September 14th in hospital. Within a few weeks, 200 people had been arrested, including trade unionists as well as unaffiliated people. On the night of June 21st, the leader of the protest, Adnan Hajji, was arrested.

The movement had been halted in its tracks. However, no women had been arrested, and so on July 27th the wives of trade unionists and activists in jail returned to the streets, demanding the release of the prisoners. Walking with them was Zakiya Dhifaoui. Born in 1966, she was a journalist and teacher. She had come from Kairouan to write a report for the opposition newspaper Muatinun, but her report was never published. Dhifaoui was arrested that day. Her arrest could be seen as a warning to all Tunisian journalists – 'don't come to Redeyef, and don't even think to write about it'. This was another facet of the repression: the censorship of any sensitive information. Dhifaoui was sentenced to four and a half months in jail, and she was not the only imprisoned journalist. It was a symbolic attack on the freedom of expression.

During the days of the event, the journalist Gabriele del Grande stopped at the Italian embassy in Tunis to seek protection after visiting Redeyef. He was aware that he'd been followed. As soon as he reached the embassy, he was met by Silvia Costantini, a young diplomat who'd arrived in Tunis after being posted to other countries with limited freedom of press. 'I'm scared. I think I've been followed,' the journalist told Silvia. She decided the young man should remain at the embassy for some time. 'You stay here, do whatever you want to do. Put some time between you and them. Whoever is following you needs to realize that we at the embassy are fully aware of the situation and that we're protecting you.' Gabriele managed to get out of the country, and his article was eventually published, but it received scant international attention, and even that died pretty soon after.

The main leaders of the Gafsa movement received very heavy sentences. One month later, Ben Ali tried to distract the public by presenting an ambitious plan to relaunch investments in Tunisia. However, according to researchers Larbi Chouikha and Vincent Geisser, memories of the protest lived in the collective minds of the people and, whether consciously or not, had set a precedent[20].

The next rumble came from France in October 2009, when the book La Regente de Carthage,[21] detailing the corruption of Leila Trabelsi, was finally published. Written by French authors Nicolas Beau and Catherine Graciet, the book documented how Leila, from her beginnings as a hairdresser, became the president's wife and power behind the throne, controlling the economic sectors and sharing this control with the rest of her family. The book did not reveal anything new to Tunisians, but it laid out proven facts of what used to be taboo or only discussed in private. Leila tried to stop the book's publication by appealing to the Parisian court, claiming that it was insulting and defamatory. The charges were rejected, however, and Leila was forced to pay €1,500 to the publishing house. Unsurprisingly, the book

---

[20] Larbi Chouikha and Vincent Geisser, « Retour sur la révolte du bassin minier. Les cinq leçons politiques d'un conflit social inédit », L'Année du Maghreb [En ligne], VI | 2010, mis en ligne le 10 juillet 2010: http://anneemaghreb.revues.org/923 ; DOI : 10.4000/anneemaghreb.923

[21] Nicolas Beau and Catherine Graciet, La régente de Carthage : Main basse sur la Tunisie, Editions La Découverte 17 September 2009.

was banned in Tunisia, but it nonetheless became quite popular thanks to Tunisians travelling to and from France. Having been published by foreigners, the book created a stir. The rest of the world learned for the first time about the situation in Tunisia, which up until then had been known only to its population.

In the summer of 2010, Ben Ali launched a press campaign targeting the 2014 elections. His intention was to bring about a change in the constitution of Tunisia by increasing the age limit of those entitled to stay in power. This came as a real shock to many Tunisians, who at the time felt Ben Ali was at the end of a cycle, and that change was therefore imminent.

On August 8th, the daily paper, Al-Chourouq, published a proclamation signed by 65 supporters, including the Olympic champion Oussama Mellouli, the media tycoon Tarek Ben Ammar, as well as doctors and lawyers. 'Tunisia still needs you!' It read. 'We need your intuition to govern the country and to ensure its future wellbeing. With this appeal we say YES to stability and continuity, which are at the base of any successful political action. We say YES to economic development, to peace, to a fair society, YES to dignity and to national sovereignty.'

In the following days, the number of signatories of this declaration reached thousands, giving life to the 'movement of the 1,000s'. Although, in 2009, there had been a page on Facebook dedicated to the '10 million Tunisians with Ben Ali,' the 'movement of the 1,000s' was still a hard blow for those hoping for possible change.

Operation WikiLeaks represented another key moment in the build-up to the revolution. Diplomatic documents, published in 2010, very clearly showed American diplomats' opinions on the authoritarian regime of Ben Ali, and they often contained harsh judgments. According to these sources from Washington, Tunisian politics were too concentrated in a single person. There was very limited freedom of press, undisputed corruption, and social problems needing urgent attention. Tunisia, the diplomats reported, should be a close US ally, but this was not the case. Even though both countries shared some fundamental values, and Tunisia's economic development was steady, its president was aging, his regime obsolete, and it was far from clear who would become his successor[22].

Many Tunisians were angry and frustrated over the evident corruption of the first lady, over the lack of jobs, and the gaping regional differences. Extremism was a constant threat, yet the Tunisian government would accept no criticism, instead imposing strict control of the country through the police. 'In one fell swoop, the candor of the cables released by Wikileaks did more for Arab democracy than decades of backstage US diplomacy,' wrote Foreign Policy[23] a few months later. This candid appraisal of Ben Ali by US diplomats showed Tunisians that the decay of the regime was obvious, not only to them, but to the whole world, and that was a source of embarrassment for the country on an international level. The cables also contradicted the prevailing view among Tunisians that Washington would back Ben Ali to the bitter end. In the end, they delegitimized the Tunisian

---

[22] Troubled Tunisia: what should we do. Op.Cit.

[23] Tom Malinowski, Whispering at Autocrats, Foreign Policy, 26 January 2011.

leader and boosted the morale of his opponents at a pivotal moment[24].

The picture would not be complete without one factor that ended up being key to the events: the global development of Tunisian information and communication technology. Among the countries of North Africa, Tunisia remains the most advanced in ICT . Indeed, it was in Tunis that the World Summit on the Information Society took place in 2005[25]. A generation of social engineers and programmers entered the employment market. The use of cell phones became widespread, extending to the most isolated areas. Along with the internet, there was also an expansion in satellite technology. The diffusion of free-to-air television channels marked a turning point in the broadcasting of information, and in the relationship between state and private television channels. At the same time, independent and well-regarded Arab channels such as Al Jazeera were launched.

However, it was social networking sites that came to play a major role, chiefly Facebook. While many websites such as YouTube were blocked, Facebook remained open, connecting people from the northern coastal city of Bizerte to the arid desert town of Tataouine. Facebook allowed Tunisians to receive un-

---

[24] Maha Azzam Opinion: How WikiLeaks helped fuel Tunisian revolution, CNN January 18, 2011. http://edition.cnn.com/2011/OPINION/01/18/tunisia.wikileaks/index.html

[25] The summit attracted 1,500 members of international organizations, 6,200 members of NGO, 4,800 people from the private sector and 980 from the media. United Nations, Report on the World Summit on the Information Society, (A/60/687), 15 March 2006.

filtered information, share texts and video clips and access unorthodox pop culture. For many people, it represented a safe virtual platform which allowed opposing views to be expressed freely, albeit sometimes via coded messages. As Le Monde was censored, and in the absence of other uncensored media, Facebook also offered Tunisians the opportunity to connect with and listen to the voices of exiled opponents. Similarly, Facebook enabled various brave advocates of regime change in the country to communicate and relay real time information to over 1 million Tunisian migrants scattered all over the world, the majority located in France, Italy and Canada.

THE SPARK THAT IGNITES

If a people want to live, then fate will answer their call.

Abou el Kacem Chebbi

December 17ᵗʰ 2010, Sidi Bouzid. This is the date that marks the start of a critical change. A desperate act becomes the symbol of protest that in less than a month will lead Tunisia to revolution.

It's a morning like any other in Sidi Bouzid, a little town of 40,000 souls in the central southern part of the country – far from the coastal resorts, holiday tours, industrial areas and motorways. Outside Tunisia, this town was known only by a handful of historians and World War II 'fanatics' who remembered the battle of Sidi Bouzid between the Germans and the Allied Forces. For us and for many others, Sidi Bouzid was no more than a place we would pass by when traveling south by car. There aren't any monuments worthy of a stop, and its name is often mixed up with the popular Sidi Bou Said, near Tunis, where millions of tourists flock every year, and where Ben Ali and his family live.

Yet the name of Sidi Bouzid is a recurrent one in Tunisian history, part of the triangle connecting Kasserine, close to the Algerian border, and Gafsa, in the south.

'The fight for independence started here,' Atiya Athmouni, a professor of philosophy and a unionist in Sidi Bouzid, told us. 'Subsequently, as it was with Bourguiba, historical events have been revised and manipulated. In later days our first revolution was claimed by northern Tunisians, who conveniently forgot about us.'

In truth, Sidi Bouzid is very remote and not easy to access. Although not far in kilometers, it can only be reached by way of an unpaved, secondary road.

The murmur of protest starts with Mohamed Bouazizi, a 26-year-old man whose father had died when he was three. Remembered by everyone as a very kind man, Mohamed finally obtained his high school diploma when he was 19. Determined to help his family, he devised a job for himself. He would wake each morning at the crack of dawn, go to buy fruit and vegetables from the central market, and resell these in one of the main squares of Sidi Bouzid. He was not licensed as a vendor but was trying to save up sufficient money to buy a new pushcart, so that he could sell his produce in the neighboring towns. 'Contrary to what people say, Mohamed had no license,' his fellow citizens told us, 'But he still represented the day-to-day struggle in an area of Tunisia hardly lauded by its citizens.'

That day, like any other day, Mohamed left very early to go to the central market, where he bought what he needed and then returned home to prepare his pushcart and make for the square. He lived ten minutes away from the town center, in a dirty street lined with rundown and unfinished houses. 'He was happy,' remembers his mother, Manoubia, welcoming us with dignity into her modest house. 'That day, he gave me one dinar (50 cents) which he'd managed to save before leaving for work.'

It is now that the episode that will dominate the front pages of newspapers worldwide takes place. Mohamed has a quarrel with a policewoman who, even though she knows him well, still asks him to show her a work license. When he refuses, she demands protection money, as well as a bag of green beans, in order to not report him. Mohamed cannot oblige. He has just bought his fruit and vegetables using a credit note, and has to sell them in order to pay off his debt. It's not the first time police have demanded that he buy a 'coupon', to be exchanged for cash which will inevitably end up in their pockets. The situation deteriorates when the policewoman decides to confiscate Mohamed's scale, and he refuses to hand it over. A fight, involving kicking and slapping, unfolds in front of other vendors and neighbors, but Mohamed's scale is valuable, and too expensive for him to redeem. The 30 dinar he will be required to pay is less than $20 US dollars, but still the equivalent of two days' work.

The international press will talk about the little cart being confiscated and about a businessman from Kuwait who offers $10,000 US dollars to buy it back. In reality, the value of the scale is less than the cart, but it's very precious to Mohamed, who decides to go to the police station to claim it back. He asks to talk to somebody and to file a complaint, but nobody at the police station is prepared to meet with him. Some witnesses report that they see him being mocked and beaten up.

The government offices are next to the police station, so Mohamed is determined to speak with the governor himself, but again his request is quickly turned down. Not even the concierge has time for him. Desperate, he buys a bottle of gasoline and, hiding it under his clothes, returns to the police station and the government offices. Once again, he begs to talk to somebody, but once again he is refused. Soaking himself with gasoline, Mohamed sets himself on fire in front of the building.

Manoubia reveals her deepest regret. 'If only someone had listened to him or convinced him to come back later ... or maybe another day ...'

This is the extreme act of a humiliated man who can see no future for himself, the extreme act of a man who wants to reclaim his karama - his dignity. 'His action was not related to the poverty in which we live, but the humiliation we suffer,' one of his neighbors tells us. 'His desire was to speak up against a dictatorial power, which refuses to allow poor people the dignity of speech.'

Tahar Ben Jelloun writes, 'this is a dramatic act with a meaning that is unambiguous and direct. Fire leaves nothing behind. It sweeps everything away and causes great pain. Mohamed didn't decide to hang himself or swallow drugs. His despair had to be translated into an act that would shock those who had been cruel and turned their backs on him. His action has gained a symbolic value, representing the desperation of an entire population. He is the victim of a regime that kills every economic, social and cultural initiative. His action represents a protest against a regime that doesn't want to face the bitter reality of its population, but hides instead behind press headlines such as "the economic miracle", together with the smiling face of the president. It's a regime that doesn't accept dialogue or self-criticism.'

A charade unfolds just moments after Mohamed's sacrifice.

'The first attempts to put out the fire are useless. The date on the fire extinguishers had expired and they were empty,' Samia Bouazizi, Mohamed's 19-year-old sister, tells us. It transpires

41

that the local bureau deceived the government and citizens by forging the expiry date on all the equipment. And the race to get him to the hospital is equally pointless, as no oxygen bottles are available. None of these details is picked up by the international press, but they clearly show the horrifying consequences of widespread corruption. Mohamed's family is forced to have him transferred to Sfax, 135 km away, in order to receive initial treatment, and the delay compromises any chance of him being saved. Meanwhile, journalist Zouhair Makhlouf is savagely attacked by the police in front of his own house as he prepares to depart for Sidi Bouzid to document what has happened.

'It was 3.00 pm as I left my house holding my camera. In front of my wife and daughter, a plainclothes policeman started to hit me with a truncheon on my face and legs. Then he stole my camera and ran away.'

Zouhair is rushed to the military hospital, suffering serious contusions on his legs, arms and face. This assault will lead to a public denunciation by Reporters Without Borders.

Night comes, but the rest of the world is still oblivious to the events.

A similar episode had played out in March of 2010, near Monastir. On that occasion, Abdesslem Trimech, another street vendor, had set himself on fire and died days later in agony. That event received next to no attention.

However, in the case of Sidi Bouzid, the images of Mohamed Bouazizi were captured by one of his friends on a cell phone and immediately shared through social media…

THE FLAMES OF PROTEST SPREAD

When the sky is red, saddle your horse and prepare to gallop.

Arab Proverb

December 18th, Sidi Bouzid/Bizerte

In Sidi Bouzid, the news of Mohamed's sacrifice spreads swiftly.

'There are four or five big families in this town. News travel fast from family to family,' says Najib Chouaibi, a professor at Kairouan University who lives in Sidi Bouzid. And those at the souk the next day continue to spread the news. 'Many vendors come from neighboring villages, and from haggling over a price, the topic quickly moves onto Mohamed's gesture, and continues onto what they should do next. People start getting together, and vendors in particular feel they're directly involved, as he was one of their own. They're often victims of violence and forced to pay protection money to the police in order to work.'

They decide to form a group and proceed to the headquarters of the local government body- raising their voices and proclaiming their unity. Police intervene to quash the protest. Many return home, angry and frustrated, both to Sidi Bouzid and to the neighboring villages, so the news spreads quickly. A short video, showing Mohamed's sacrifice, appears on YouTube on December 18th, but is immediately censored all over Tunisia. Facebook then plays a pivotal role in broadcasting the video, which starts to spread, not only in Sidi Bouzid, but also among Tunisians living abroad, who can easily access sites blocked in Tunisia and pass on the news without fear of imprisonment. And so, the news bounces from abroad back to Tunisia. It's Imen Chorfi, aged 20, who tells us how people became aware of events by way of the most unusual channels. We got to know Imen, a biochemical student in Bizerte, by accident. We were looking on Facebook for a different person who shared her name, and she accepted our request out of kindness.

'I received the video through Facebook via a friend who came from Sidi Bouzid, but lives in France. He was then informed by somebody else, who filmed the event on his cell phone.' Imen does not outwardly show her distress, but central to her thoughts is that this is a replay of the first immolation in Monastir. Imen continues, 'At that time I didn't know, nor was I interested in, the reasons that pushed Mohamed Bouazizi to set himself on fire, but then, talking to a friend, I felt sympathy for this young man who, although very poor, tried to do something. Unlike other young people from my country who are happy enough to sit about in a café, waiting for someone to offer them a job, Mohamed tried everything at any cost. I think this is the main reason why many people identify with this man. He didn't try to set himself on fire because he could not get a job, but because the job he created for himself was snatched from him with such force.'

In the meantime, the protest spreads quickly, and in the days following, police use tear gas. The first posts appear on Twitter, where a new stream called Sidi Bouzid is created, and where the entire world is able to follow the events as they unfold One of the very first tweets is in English, using the codename ifikra, 'Internet connection has been blocked in Sidi Bouzid because of the protests, and also in Birmania and Iran,' it reads. Nine minutes later, another tweet flashes up from @karim2k, who writes, 'The city of Sidi Bouzid is in rebellion. Please help to promote the Hashtag' (the symbol # placed before a key word).

In the coming days, the #SidiBouzid hashtag has more than 100,000 tweets. This is the power of information spread by word of mouth and made available via new technologies. Of course, it's picked up by the Tunisian government, which tries to block access by isolating Sidi Bouzid. Too late. The message has already gone flying across the ocean.

Alaeddine Ben Abdallah, a university professor in Ottawa, was initially skeptical about the possibility of protests overcoming government repression, after witnessing the events in Redeyef two years earlier. Now, he starts spreading the news with a vigor fueled by outrage. 'For the first time a protest has reached outside the city, and this means it won't be so easily suppressed.' His friends warn him about the risks, but the professor, equipped with his keyboard, starts a dedicated assault. Using Facebook, Twitter and his blog, he launches appeals to support the revolution. Al Jazeera, too, becomes the leading channel to break the news. Apart from France Presse, international media is slow to understand the importance of these events. Al Jazeera, however, grasps the symbolic significance and is the first to broadcast the early videos sourced by witnesses. Bassam Sebti, an American journalist, writes on his blog, 'America was founded on the principles of liberty and freedom, but guess who was covering the quest for freedom in Tunisia extensively yesterday? Not the American news TV networks! Al Jazeera!' As one of the most popular messages on Twitter stated, 'While Al Jazeera is following the events in

Tunisia, MSNBC is busy broadcasting news relating to Martha Stewart's dog.'

A RAPPER CHALLENGES THE HYPOCRISY OF THE REGIME

Falsehood has an infinity of combinations, but truth had only one mode of being.

Jean-Jacques Rousseau

December 19th, Tunis

It's been two days since Mohamed Bouazizi's sacrifice, and the Tunisian press is still silent. La Presse, the most widely read daily paper, makes no mention of it. Instead, the front pages are filled with articles about the first anniversary of the International Year of Youth, initiated by Ben Ali, including numerous celebrities paying him homage for supporting young people. In the paper, owned by Ben Ali's son-in-law, there is an article addressed to the president from a group of youngsters. They express their sincere gratitude to him for paying particular attention to the city of Sidi Hassine, where the celebrations are taking place, thanking him for his constant and ready support of its inhabitants, –particularly the young. The article emphasizes the devotion they feel to Ben Ali for his commitment to leading Tunisia towards progress and prosperity.

'This exasperating hypocrisy shows the disdain for the martyred lad, and for everyone else,' says Z, a dissident cartoonist who for years has been illegally publishing sketches and cartoons on his blog, DEBAtunisie. His statement is accompanied by a portrait of Ben Ali preparing for the youth day. In it, he uses a lighter to ignite a candle in the shape of a boy on top of a cake. Z's daring pen has given the esteemed president a thunderous expression. His face is blackened by smoke, symbolic of a regime that, by trying to eliminate all opposition, is in fact destroying itself by fire.

This image is picked up and published by the Belgian paper, Le Soir. Z writes, 'this terrible story is the rerun of what happened in Monastir last year, when a young man, Abdesslem Trimech, dowsed himself in petrol and burned himself alive outside the Municipality Buildings. In both cases the indifference of the authorities forced these lads to kill themselves. Their suicides, right outside government buildings, represent the most extreme form of political protest against the symbols of power. Their sacrifices are also a potent instrument to alert public opinion.'

Z claims the regime is running scared. After the initial demonstrations in Sidi Bouzid, officials have blocked internet all over the city, intending to stop the broadcasting of any video showing the security forces in action. This strategy is adopted a few weeks later, on a larger scale, in Egypt by President Mubarak. It proves to be equally futile.

Hamada Ben Amor is a 22-year-old man who goes by the pseudonym 'El General.' It is he who launches the ultimate attack against the regime, and his weapon of choice is a hip-hop song. His songs express the frustrations of his compatriots, while encouraging young people to respond peacefully. The song Rais Lebled (the head of the country) speedily gets aired, and becomes an anthem for many. It's a direct attack on the president, which describes him as shivering in his shoes.

'The President asks a child, 'Why are you preoccupied? Have you got something you want to tell me?'

The child's response, representing Tunisian youth, is translated into a rap.

'People are treated like animals; the police are monsters speaking only with their batons. Mr. President, you told me to speak without fear, but I know that eventually, I shall take only slaps. I see too much injustice, so I have decided to send this message, even though the people tell me that it will end in my death. For how much longer must Tunisians live in fear? Where is their freedom of expression?'

These words are unambiguous, and alongside Mohamed's desperate act, they quickly become a rallying cry for young people. Maybe Mohamed's fate would have been different had he held a microphone instead of a canister of gasoline, but the union of these two gestures touches people.

A BLOODY CHRISTMAS

Do not suffer the vicissitudes of the moment.
Beyond the darkness there is a new dawn.
Without the cloudy sky of an angry winter
The garden can produce such a beautiful mantle of flowers.
Abou el Kacem Chebbi

December 24th, Rome/London/Menzel Bouzaiane
It's Christmas, and we are in Europe celebrating the holidays. Like many expats, we have left Tunisia totally unaware of what is happening. Many Tunisians are also on holiday. Although the vast majority of Tunisia's population is Muslim, everything slows down during the Christian holidays. Many expats return to their home countries. Tunisians born into mixed marriages also return to their families in Europe and North America.

Sofien is one of them. He is 30 years old and works for an international organization based in Tunisia. His father is Tunisian and his mother French. He left Tunisia with his family when he was 14 to move to Washington DC, and 16 years later he returned to Tunis, after having been offered a prestigious job back in his home country. He was looking forward to returning to his roots and to experiencing his own culture.

Before leaving the USA, his father warned him, 'Be careful of what you say and to whom you say it.' At the time Sofien was surprised, although he remembered how, during past summers, his cousins and friends would become nervous whenever he attempted to talk about politics.

Once in Tunis, he's eager to express his views, despite his father's repeated warnings to avoid Tunisian politics. His colleagues, however, repeatedly seek his opinions. On Christmas Eve, Sofien is at home with his parents and two brothers, who live in Paris and London, celebrating Christmas. This is a tradition kept alive by his Catholic mother. Here, at home, he can talk freely.

'My brothers ask me what's happening in Tunis, and I tell them the few facts I know. As I say that, I realize how little I do know of what is going on. My brothers are far more informed, living as they do in London and Paris, than I, in Tunis. They've followed the chain of events initiated by Mohamed Bouazizi's suicide and the protests in the different areas of the country. Only then do I realize that I'm seeing only the tip of the iceberg,' explains Sofien. 'My brothers can also recall the events that happened in Redeyef in 2008, and they're convinced that this protest will be equally useless and will eventually be repressed.'

Nevertheless, the riots continue, expanding beyond Sidi Bouzid, to the south and the center of the country. The reactions of the police become increasingly violent. The first victim is Mohamed Ammari, who is 18 years old and is shot in Menzel Bouzaiane, 60 km from Sidi Bouzid. This is not an isolated case. Chawki Belhoussine El Hadri is shot during the same protest. He dies a few days later. The police don't bother with tear gas, and use real bullets, not hesitating to fire at the protesters. The Minister of the Interior justifies these instances as acts of self-defense by the police who, it is claimed, feel threatened by the angry protesters. Further clashes between the authorities and rioters occur in the cities of Al Ragab and Meknassi, both in the region of Sidi Bouzid. News of the initial confrontation and first fatality is patchy. Aside from a short mention on Euronews, Facebook offers the most easily accessible line of communication, broadcasting videos and evidence filmed by Al Jazeera and the BBC.

Tunisian events are still widely absent from world news. Owing to the silence of the media, Menzel Bouzaiane suffers. The police go as far as encircling the city, allowing nobody to enter or leave. In the evening, the silence is broken by Moez El Bey, a correspondent with Radio Kaliema ('word,' in Arabic), an independent Tunisian station which has been censored in Tunisia for many years but still broadcasts using international radio frequencies. Moez El Bey is in his house in Tunis, connected to Marsiglia 88.4 via Radio Galera. After a few minutes devoted to the events of Menzel Bouzaiane, the broadcast is suddenly interrupted by banging on his door and screaming. Then the line is abruptly cut off.

The next day, what happened to Moez El Bey is reported to the world on Nawaat.org, a Tunisian blog. Following the instructions of the police, his neighbors bashed in his door and attacked him. This time, the authorities have delegated their dirty work to unidentified people. Even so, aggression can't halt the stream of information finally under way. Videos appear on Facebook and on Rue89.com showing, for the first time, pictures and posters of the president being set on fire by angry protesters. It's certainly a different sort of Christmas.

THE WORLD 'WAKES UP'

> *You should have fed the wolves.*
> *They will lie in ambush in the forest.*
> Slogan of Tunisian protest in Paris.

December 25th, Paris/California

The protests spread to the major cities in central Tunisia. There are demonstrations in Kairouan, one of the most holy cities in the country, in Sfax, the economic capital, and in Ben Gardane on the Libyan border. Nothing has happened in Tunis, the political and administrative capital, but a demonstration of people originally from Sidi Bouzid and other parts of the nation takes place in Paris, in the 20th Arrondissement (the eastern part of the capital). This is a cosmopolitan neighborhood, which has housed immigrants since 1850. Walls in the area are covered with slogans on the Tunisian Revolution – 'Algeria, Tunisia, Yes to Rebellion!' 'Sarko, Ben Ali and others – we won't forget or forgive.' 'You should have fed the wolves, as now they will lie in ambush in the forest.'

The following day it's the turn of the 16th Arrondissement, home to the Tunisian Consulate. A group of people fight the cold, jumping from one foot to the other, hiding frozen faces inside the collars of their coats. They are responding actively to the appeal of solidarity from the demonstrators in Sidi Bouzid. Some people shout, 'Ben Ali ala barra barra!' ('Ben Ali out!' in Arabic). Hands clap in unison and slogans abound. Microphones in hand, demonstrators such as Moheiddine Cherib, Omeyya Seddik and Adel Thabet address the crowd. 'The only way to launch an appeal in Tunisia today is to commit suicide. People are forced to kill themselves in order to be rid of Ben Ali and his clan. We demand that Ben Ali resigns. Then we shall forgive him for everything he's done. He must hand over the power to those who deserve it. Meanwhile, we shall carry on protesting until we see change.'

Omeyya Seddik urges Tunisians to take this chance to change the social, economic and political situation of the country. At the same time, Moheiddine Cherib points out how the number of demonstrators in front of the Tunisian Consulate has increased each day.

Across the ocean on Christmas Eve, Joe Sullivan, Facebook's chief security officer, notices a strange coincidence. Complaints by different users proliferate in direct correlation to the protest – related Facebook pages are being deliberately scrambled. After an investigation which lasts 10 days, Sullivan and his partners realize that providers in Tunisia are attacking the site in order to steal users' passwords. Their immediate reaction is to divert the access onto an https server, which is safer than the normal http one. Other protection systems are activated. The government, which originally accepted Facebook, becomes increasingly aware of its dangerous potential and tries to block the spread of information. While the president meets with the Tunisian governor of Tunisia's central bank, Nawaat.org broadcasts information revealing that the presidential plane is getting ready to depart for Dubai.

'A strange message,' comments Arabies, a popular magazine in the Arab world.

THE LAWYERS ON THE FRONT LINE

Awake, justice – a hairdresser commands you!
Slogan of the lawyers' demonstration

December 27ᵗʰ, Tunis/Rome
In Tunis, it's the first day back at work after the short Christmas break.

'Are you aware of what's happening?' asks Saoussen, one of our closest Tunisian friends.

She is visibly excited. Meanwhile, the government newspapers continue to publish the same old propaganda, most Tunisians avoid talking politics, and the high number of policemen on the streets gives the illusion that everything is under control.

Saoussen continues, 'A man set himself on fire, and the country is flooded with protests led by lawyers.' 'Lawyers!' We wonder naively, accustomed to student- or union-run protests in the West. 'Since when did lawyers initiate protests?'

However, it's no coincidence that lawyers are the first professional group to organize demonstrations in support of the youngsters in Sidi Bouzid.

'Our profession has managed to retain the right to elect its own representatives,' Soumaya Ben Abderrahmene, a lawyer and Tunisian activist, explains to us a few days later.

Even though there are considerable imbalances, caused by different conditions, financial restraints and government interference- numerous political affiliations are present among lawyers: there are laics, Islamists, pro-regime supporters, and members of the opposition. They all have a voice in lawyers' associations.

'The members of the lawyers' association remained united against Bourguiba and against Ben Ali, and fought against the subjugation of justice,' writes Alya Cherif Chammari, another lawyer. He calls the lawyers 'the real architects of the revolution'. The lawyers' active participation had actually started a few years earlier, during the riots in the mining basin around Gafsa. Back then, a group of them had joined the demonstrators, demanding the right to a fair trial and opposing the blatant disregard for human rights by the authorities. But once the lawyers had returned to Tunis, they faced several difficulties. Some found that their car engines were filled with sand, some that they were denied bookings in restaurants, while others discovered that they were no longer allowed to leave the city – and so on. It was a long line of petty and malicious abuses of power, intended to demonstrate just who was in control. However, the dearest price to pay was that they could no longer take part in any important trials, were barred from government jobs, and were subjected to 'extra' scrutiny by the Tunisian tax authorities.

Lawyers were effectively split into two main camps. On one side were the privileged 200 – those who supported the government – on the other, the 7,000 (called *Corsairs* by Soumaya) who faced various difficulties, including having to work exclusively from home, but who steadfastly supported the people.

On December 27th, the Order of Council organizes a sit-in dedicated to the demonstrators in Sidi Bouzid, to take place in the Palace of Justice. Soumaya, like many others, anticipates fresh arrests – similar to what happened a few years earlier in

Gafsa. However, probably because of the number of individual movements that have arisen spontaneously since Mohamed Bouazizi's immolation, the police make no move. In Soumaya's opinion, 'Now is the time to change. Now they must take action.'

She arrives at her office, situated near Avenue Bourguiba, one of Tunisia's central avenues, early in the morning. She parks her car and gathers up her lawyer's robe. Thinking that it will be difficult to reach the Palace of Justice, she decides to take a detour through the souk, but on the other side of the market, she encounters a cordon of policemen asking people for their identification documents. Undeterred, she produces her robe. 'I'm a lawyer, and I'm about to join a demonstration.' Incredibly, she is let through and proceeds to the Palace of Justice. There, she finds the police are more organized. They have dogs and vans waiting. After some time, the group of lawyers continues on to the main office, located on the other side of the road. One or two of them climb on to chairs and address the crowd, like orators. Among them, Soumaya notices Abdraouf Ayadi and Chockri Belaid, both famous for their defense of human rights. These two are leading the protest.

Amazingly, everything passes peacefully, and the police don't arrest anyone. The crowd disperses – Soumaya returns to work.

At 5.00 pm, the phone rings. Some out-of-uniform officers have arrested Abdraouf Ayadi and taken him away. Soumaya's heart sinks. How many more demonstrators will be arrested? She seizes the telephone and calls all the people she knows. She manages to make contact with everyone except Chockri Belaid.

Chockri's cell phone is ringing, but there's no answer. Since the start of the demonstrations, all the lawyers have adopted new codes of behavior. Mobile phones are switched on at all times, and always answered. But Chocki does not pick up, and further calls confirm that he left his office 15 minutes earlier. Soumaya's worst suspicions have been confirmed. Chockri, too, has been arrested.

Soumaya returns to the head office to discover that her colleagues have already gathered there. Someone calls the Minister of Justice and the Interior to seek confirmation of the arrests; nobody picks up the phone, and when they do finally make contact, no one bothers to reply for an hour and a half. After a fraught period of collective anxiety, however, they receive confirmation that the two activists have been arrested and are, at that moment, being interrogated.

This is the instant when the lawyers are galvanized into action. Their first move is to contact Al Jazeera, followed by every radio station and television outlet to which they have access. Then they set about contacting other bodies of lawyers worldwide. Perhaps as a result of the widespread condemnation that follows, both Ayadi and Belaid are released the next day, although Ayadi has been tortured. Images of his back, crisscrossed with whipping marks, are relayed around the world.

It is on December 27th that people in the south of the country start their protest. Their demonstrations spread to Sousse and inevitably on to Tunis.

A thousand young graduates who have been unable to find employment organize a demonstration in support of the protestors nationwide. For the first time, the north and the south of the country appear united in revolt.

THE PRESIDENT'S RESPONSE

You who insist in your arrogance!
Shut up, you who tread on shattered skulls!
Don't hurry; in the moans of those crushed
Underfoot, there is an awesome voice whose echo will spread.
Abou el Kacem Chebbi

December 28ᵗʰ, Tunis/Gafsa/Montreal
Under pressure following the protests, Ben Ali agrees to talk to the media. His first move is to visit Mohamed Bouazizi, who has been transferred to the burns unit of Ben Arous Hospital, just outside Tunis. He is depicted in a surreal photograph, posing with Bouazizi, who is bandaged like an Egyptian mummy and surrounded by doctors[26].

A few weeks later, Bouazizi's mother tells us, 'It was pathetic. Ben Ali remained at my son's bedside just long enough to have one photograph taken. Afterwards, he met my daughter and me at his palace. When he emerged from my son's hospital room, all he said was, "What am I going to do with this one?" That is the real nature of our president; showing a courteous exterior, but inside having nothing but contempt for his people.'

---

[26] President Zine al Abidine Ben Alivisits young man Mohamed Bouazizi, Tunisia Tour, 28 December 2010, www.tunisia-tour/fr/tunisie/tunisia-news/1078-president-zine-el-abidine-ben-ali-visits-young-man-mohamed-bouazizi, retrieved 23 January 2011.

In the evening, Ben Ali addresses the nation on television. He speaks for seven minutes. His speech is broadcast to the entire Arab world by way of Al Jazeera. Three and a half minutes in, his speech descends into chaos. His cell phone starts to ring. Ben Ali does not pick up the phone, but attempts to speak over the insistent tone, all the while staring at the instrument. He looks visibly stressed and foolish.

Meanwhile Haichem, a 39-year-old freelance journalist, is sitting in a bar in Tunis. He commutes between Tunis and Kairouan, and, after a long day at work, slips into the bar to enjoy a shisha. It is is packed, and there is only standing room as people gather to see the president and hear what he has to say.

'People never talk politics in bars,' Haichem reports, 'They're scared, because there are too many spies about. This is the first time I have ever heard people comment on Ben Ali. In their opinion, his speech was a total failure, and all their talk was critical. "He said not one new word," and, "Is this his only reply?" people comment.'

The bar becomes empty, the patrons continuing to criticize the seven-minute speech as they depart for their homes. Jokes are exchanged. 'Who rang the president at that precise moment? Why was he afraid to answer his phone? Perhaps he feared it might bite him'. Up until that moment, such comments were unheard of in a Tunisian bar. This was a sign that something was changing.

Facebook and Twitter quickly become a virtual bar where critical remarks are widely shared. Haichem says, 'The combination of that ringing cell phone, his dyslexia and the pathetic nature of his patriarchal speech supporting freedom! What a farce.

61

I'd have preferred to watch *Club Africain* playing football. Far more entertaining.'

Despite this, there are people, such as Mohamed, whose opinions differ. In his opinion, unemployment is a worldwide problem, affecting rich countries as well as poor. Instead of criticizing, he says people should be trying to solve these difficulties.

'I agree with you,' replies Nahla. 'Unemployment is an international problem, the difference being that in other countries people are not forced to commit suicide because of it.'

'Ben Ali's speech was a lost opportunity,' writes Brian Whitaker on his blog. 'A clever dictator would have come up with some initiatives to combat the crisis, but Ben Ali said nothing original, nothing that hasn't already been said. He asked people not to waste time, and urged government officials to do their best and take responsibility; at the same time arguing that there is unemployment in other countries, too. According to Ben Ali, protests triggered by Bouazizi's suicide are understandable, but at the same time they have been used as a means by enemies and television channels to defame the country, dramatizing the facts and making false accusations. His words sounded like a threat. According to him, these protests against unemployment end up damaging unemployed people, because they discourage investors and tourists. He then went on to promise to use the law against extremists and those who jeopardize the image of Tunisia abroad.'

'Ben Ali's speech demonstrated his blunders quite clearly,' writes Thierry Meyssan, a political analyst. 'Instead of talking calmly to his people and soothing their fears, Ben Ali called the protestors extremists and announced his intention to repress the demonstrations, which will transform protests into riots. Tunisians are now committed to fighting against social injustice, but above all against extreme political power.'

Trades unions announce a demonstration to take place in Gafsa, but this protest is killed off by the authorities before it even begins. Meanwhile, a group of 300 lawyers assembles before the Government Palace in Tunis.

In a desperate effort to lay the blame on somebody, the central government dismisses the governors of Sidi Bouzid, Jendouba and Zaghouan.

Simultaneously, through Twitter, Tunisians living in the area organize a demonstration in front of the Tunisian Consulate in Montreal. Thanks to their dynamism, Tunisians living in Canada create 'a continuum of protests, from one side of the country to the other.'

The following day, Rym, a young lawyer, finds herself sitting in the Business Lounge at Tunis Airport. Rym's office is located close to the Tunis city center, and her job is to assist any foreigners wishing to invest in Tunisia. She is about to fly to Berlin, where she will spend the New Year break.

She recalls, 'Businessmen were whispering amongst themselves, talking about the ongoing protests, but above all the talk was about Ben Ali's visit to Mohamed. For a western leader, this visit would be seen as an act of compassion and solidarity. Not so for Ben Ali; normally, he goes nowhere. There must be some other motive behind his action.'

Rym, like most others, is unaware of what is happening in the south. She rarely bothers to read the local papers, filled as they are with propaganda. But now, sitting in the lounge at the airport, she reaches for a copy of *La Presse* and stares at the picture of Ben Ali standing beside the bed of Mohamed Bouazizi. She describes her reaction to the photograph as one of bitterness and sadness.

Francesca Bellino, a journalist and writer, has always followed Tunisian events with interest. She is married to a Tunisian actor, Ahmed Hafiene. Today, she is also traveling. She is at Frankfurt Airport in Germany. As she waits for her flight, for the first time she reads an article about the ongoing demonstrations. The article, published in La Repubblica and written by Alberta Flores d'Arcais, describes the anger of young Tunisians, the discontent of unemployed people, and the disregard for human rights. 'People don't want bread, as many in the media claim,' writes d'Arcais, 'but they do want their dignity restored.'

Francesca explains, 'Reading this article at that precise moment made me realize that even the sleepy Italian press had started to take some interest in the Tunisian protests. Right then, on my way to Prague, my heart started to beat faster, and I bombarded myself with questions. Somehow, I discover I'm also on fire within. I'm sure that 2011 will see the courage and the determination of all Tunisians come to fruition. I think about Prague and Sidi Bouzid, I think about the 1969 revolution and compare it with December 17th in Tunisia – but mostly my mind is on Mohamed Bouazizi, who could become the Arab Jan Palech, and who like him protested by self-immolation. I'm filled with inspiration, and I decide then and there to write a novel, set in Tunisia. I open my handbook and quickly transcribe the opening sentences of the story.'

THE REVOLTS GO ON TV

If you halt every time a dog barks,
you will never complete your walk.

Arab proverb

December 30ᵗʰ, Tunis

Monique, a Belgian expat who has lived in Tunisia for twenty years, thinks to herself that this is a special day. She is heading towards Bab Dzira, a key area in Tunis, only accessible by foot and a short distance from the medina (the old town). It's a popular area, because it's sufficiently far from patrolling police and the perfect place to stage a demonstration. A post on an activist website has marked each geographic area of the nation where demonstrations are scheduled to take place simultaneously. At least, this is until the site is closed down. Through Facebook, 640 people have signaled their intention to gather at Bab Dzira. The mastermind behind this invitation is Houeida Anouar, who has scrambled the message on both Facebook and Twitter.

Asma, a 22-year-old law student, is also on her way to Bab Dzira Square. But before she can arrive, she is spotted by a policeman. He tries to stop her. Asma tells us, 'All the police know who I am; and they know I'm an activist. I've already been questioned.'

As Monique approaches the square, she is confronted by more than 100 policemen, facing 20 demonstrators. It's an impossible situation! The demonstrators are fully aware that this

65

time they have been thwarted. They pretend that they are only there to meet with friends and leave in small groups of four and five. Several people join Monique, then they stroll through the medina, and stop at one of the tourist cafés opposite the Porte de France (French Gate) – the main tourist area. Ten policemen follow their steps. It's a terrifying moment. Monique and her companions continue to chat in a lively manner about everything except the intended demonstration. A second group of would-be demonstrators appears. They are stopped by the police and questioned, and it appears that one young man's answers are seen as hostile and sarcastic. In response, the police take out their sticks and beat him in front of his friends, who are helpless to intervene. All the bystanders can do is witness the event.

'Around dinnertime, that evening,' Monique tells us, 'we receive a text message from a friend, telling us to switch to Nessma (a TV channel) at 7:30 pm. They will be showing a program about Sidi Bouzid.'

Nessma is the first private satellite TV exclusive to the Maghreb. It has about 90 million viewers, which includes 6 million in North Africa and France, and 2 million in Italy[27]. Nessma was launched in 2007 by a Tunisian-based advertizing group and subsequently financed by the French-Tunisian TV tycoon Tarak Ben Ammar, the Mediaset Group owned by Italian tycoon and Prime Minister Silvio Berlusconi, who also happened to be Tarak Ben Ammar's long-time friend. Nessma (literally 'sweet breeze') is an all-embracing channel with a focus on entertain-

---

[27] North Africa journal, 18 February 2011. www.north-africa.com/social.../2febtwenty46.html

ment[28]. The main office is in Tunis, where it's known as 'Berlusconi's own TV' and considered to take little interest in genuine issues. Instead, it features beautiful women, dancing, sport lookalikes and American programs (the most famous being a sort of Tunisian 'American Idol', in which talent-spotters abound). Real news is almost non-existent.

'Our decoder has been broken for weeks,' Monique continues, 'And is still with the technician who should have mended it ages ago. Even so, the internet is a reasonable alternative. We're able to see the video uploaded a few hours after the end of the program; and we can also access Facebook and Twitter's 'Virtual Tribunals,' which are filled with comments. Nessma actually invited several journalists onto the program, who are known to be critical of the government and its actions. This has never happened before!'

Among them is Bochra Belhadj Hamida, a human rights' activist who appears for the first time ever on a Tunisian TV channel. The inhabitants of Sidi Bouzid are able to talk freely about the problems facing this remote and (compared to the coastal resorts) neglected region - its lack of infrastructure and services, and the difficulty of finding work and supporting one's family. By broadcasting this program, Nessma has broken the self-imposed censorship rules followed by all Tunisian news media – it has mentioned the demonstrations at length, and gone so far as to talk about the potential transition towards democracy. The message given is very clear – this system is not working.

---

[28] Mediaset rotta sul nord Africa, 22 May 2008. http://argomenti.ilsole24ore.com/nessma.html

'We have reached the point of no return; Tunisia is changing,' writes Nizar on Twitter.

'I cannot understand how we can be part of media manipulation, giving a wrong and hypocritical image of Tunisia,' adds a user under a pseudonym.

'The entire show was aimed at attacking Al Jazeera and government channels, rather than talking about the real problems that this country is facing,' writes Amel on Twitter. Clearly, there is quite a lot of interest engendered by this issue, even though two weeks have now passed. The intention is to gain credibility without exaggeration of the facts, and eventually prepare for the post-Ben Ali period.

Nessma TV is in fact very popular with young people, but like every other channel, it is considered pro-regime. At the time of Ben Ali's political campaign, it aired a long advertisement supporting the President's re-election, disregarding candidates belonging to the opposition party. Immediately after the elections, Tarek Ben Ammar took part in a press briefing, where he described Ben Ali as the only valid candidate for the elections of 2014, subject to constitutional change. Ben Ammar's name was among the 65 signatories of the list that stated, 'Tunisia still needs you.'

Still, Ben Ammar is not among the thousands who, 12 days later, took part in the 'patriotic initiative', this time orchestrated by Mohamed Sakher El Materi, the anticipated heir, and many other businessmen, such as the General Secretary of the Confederation of Tunisian Industry, lawyers, heads of unions, bankers and students.

Ben Ammar is close to Ben Ali but not necessarily to his extended family – a subtle but important difference. The same can be said for Nessma's general director, Fahmi Huwaidi, a member of the RCD since 1964. He held the position of Secretary of State for Information during the media blackout ordered by Ben Ali in the 1990s, but has become more of a fringe player in recent years. In fact, Huwaidi is in collision with Ben Ali's supporters, such as his long-time rival Abdul Wahab Abdullah, the president's political counselor and the former Minister of Foreign Affairs.

One freelance reporter who asked for anonymity states, 'Nessma's program is not an attempt to take part in any revolution that has little chance of succeeding, but it's a way to show the divisions in Ben Ali's own party, and it's also an attempt by Huwaidi to decry Ben Ali's supporters, by denouncing his excesses.'

The game is still on.

THE 'MICRO-INTELLECTUALS' RALLY

Mankind divides into three groups; the immovable, the movable, and those that move others.

Arab proverb

January 1ˢᵗ, Sidi Bou Said/ La Marsa

Hela, who is 28, describes herself as a geek – someone whose passion for information technology and digital communication goes beyond a simple hobby. In a sector dominated by men, it's unusual to find a woman with such a passion. One of the first Twitter users in Tunisia, Hela has sent over 4,000 tweets, and she has more than 2,000 followers who regularly receive her messages on their phones. Like so many Tunisians, she lived abroad for a period, (in her case in France) and it was from there that she started her opposition, using the telephone and tweets to good effect. The blog site she launched was rapidly censored and blocked by the government, but this did not stop her from writing articles, although deemed illegal, that were aired on a virtual platform used by protestors...

Until 2003, Hela used to write under a pseudonym, but she then decided to use her own name. It was a few months after this change that she came home to Tunisia, to attend her brother's funeral. On the day she attempted to return to France, however, the police took her passport at the border control, 'inviting' her to collect it again from the Ministry of the Interior.

'Who are your associates?' she was asked. 'What you write is subversive and illegal.'

Hela discovered that they were fully informed about her writing at the Ministry. She was not tortured, for which she was thankful, but she was told to sign a document declaring that her writing was defamatory and untrue. When she refused to sign, her passport was withheld, and she was unable to leave Tunisia.

'My country has become my prison,' says Hela. 'A prison that's 16,000 square kilometers.'

During her enforced stay in the country, Hela admits that she lost her enthusiasm for the fight. She became disappointed in her fellow countrymen, who, in her perception, had abandoned the battle and lost the will to challenge the situation.

'My anger against the regime morphed into sadness,' she says. She entered a phase of 'slack-tivism' (slackness and passive activism), doing no more than spreading information, and deliberately stepping back from center stage. She did, however, stay in touch with web protestors living abroad.

'I've been in contact with a large community for many years,' she explains. 'I communicate with many whose faces I don't know.' It is in this way that she gets in touch with Karim, one of many web friends, with whom she decides to organize an open meeting for all activists living in Tunis. Twenty brave people arrive at her house in Sidi Bou Said, the wealthy neighborhood near the capital. They discuss the current situation in the country, and exchange ideas about names and possible slogans for their group.

'We need a tagline,' says Karim, employing Twitter terminology – a tagline being a short sentence that will instantly clarify the aim and meaning of the protest.

On January 1st, the sun is shining, and in the well-to-do neighborhoods to the north of Tunis – from Gammarth to Carthage – people buzz with the new initiatives they hear about at both secret and publicly-held meetings. They attend lunches, where alcohol is served and the abundant food includes pork and other pork-based products. Many Tunisians are eager to reclaim the joys of eating and drinking.

Malek says, smiling, 'If God is kind, why does he forbid us to eat delicious food such as pork?'

A group of friends gathers at Hatem's house in La Marsa. Hatem is a Tunisian banker who has organized a last-minute New Year's party. Most of the guests are Tunisian, with the exception of ourselves – the Italians – a French couple, and a German man whose wife is Tunisian. Most of the talk centers around the program about Sidi Bouzid aired on Nessma. Interestingly, the major topic of discussion is about the poverty they have seen in Sidi Bouzid, rather than the debate about democracy.

'I would never have imagined such poverty existed in Tunisia. It's a disgrace,' exclaims Saoussen, who wonders how the media has managed to hide this reality for so many years.

Tarik, who hails from Kasserine, another very poor area, continues, 'We're ashamed to be seen living in such conditions.' He is speaking in French, and when he realizes that the French guests are looking at him, he switches to Arabic, which is one way to exclude strangers from such a delicate subject.

The conversation heats up. 'It's time to do something!' Kamel's impatience is reflected in his voice. Kamel is a blogger and has taken part in protests since he was a member of the General Students' Union, which has a history of opposing the regime. In his opinion, it's time to take the protest to the streets.

Dissenting voices can be heard pointing out that this is not the right time because there is no obvious leader behind whom protestors can unite. Other guests point out that this is the strength of the present movement, because this very fact – that there is no individual and charismatic leader – means there is no clash of interests. Instead, the aspirations of all social classes, from lawyers to the masses, can be heard.

We foreigners decide to slip off. We make our way towards Hatem's balcony, which has a spectacular view of the sea, to enjoy the sunset. We also want to respect the privacy of those who are discussing the future of their country.

Simultaneously, as we enjoy the fiery end of the day, on Facebook, the argument is heating up. It's mostly initiated by young hotheads who resent those who take up valuable time and space by posting beautiful but useless images of the New Year – in their opinion they should be utilizing the site as a platform for the current unrest.

In the south, while new and bloody protests are beginning, a small elite group of young and rich citizens debate among themselves how to tackle future communication. Because at present there is no spearhead of intellectuals in the vanguard, the activists know that they must rely for communication upon Twitter and Facebook. Fortunately, many people can be reached via these sites. Hela calls them 'micro-intellectuals.' Each tweet of 140 characters can be accessed by many thousands of people, not only in Tunisia, but also around the world.

ANONYMOUS VS. BEN ALI

*The bright star shines again and the stagnant clouds are ob-
scured.*
Abou el Kacem Chebbi

January 2nd, Tunis

'Today, more than 9,000 'hacktivists' get together to show
their support for fellow Tunisians,' writes Houeida, a young
blogger. 'And the result is that the government's website
crashes! Ati.tn and bawaba.gov.tn are the first two casualties. Go
to #operationtunisia to follow the cybernetic war against oppression and censorship!'

This marks the day of the International Web Pirates revolt,
and in particular the influence of Anonymous, a leaderless movement which has been working for some time against any forms
of internet censorship. Anonymous takes part in the Tunisian
Revolution without physically being there, and on
anonnews.org, it invites people to take up the same challenge.
Anonymous.org is a free space used by web activists to share information. The message that appears on the site is very clear.

'The moment for truth has arrived. It is time for people to
express themselves freely and to be heard all around the world.
The Tunisian Government wants to control Today with lies and
misinformation, in order to impose itself on Tomorrow, by keeping the truth hidden from its citizens.'

A few hours later, the same movement launches a hitherto unattempted attack. It scrambles all the government websites, while simultaneously publishing a letter addressed to the Tunisian Government and spread via Anonymous.org. 'We have been monitoring your treatment of your own citizens, and we are greatly saddened and enraged by your behavior. You have unilaterally declared war on free speech, democracy and even your people. Your citizens rally in the streets to demand accountability and their rights, which you have wrongfully assumed to be yours to take from them.' the letter continues with what can be seen as a portend: 'Remember that the more tightly you squeeze your citizens, the more they will rebel against your rule. Like a fistful of sand in the palm of your grip, the tighter you squeeze your people, the faster they will flow from your grasp. The more you censor them, the more they will investigate you, and discover how you behave.'

In the face of Tunisia's aggressive censorship, Anonymous is able to provide a protected alternative outlet of expression, and Nawaat.org goes further, offering technical information for protection against police attacks. USB software, which allows for writer anonymity, is distributed. This is war.

Jack is part of the Anonymous team. He's a young American researcher who has lived in Tunis for several years, having won a scholarship to study 'The Tunisian Paradox'. This basically refers to the conundrum in which the more people seek and gain tertiary education, the greater the unemployment rates climb. It took Jack a very short time to become deeply frustrated by the iron-fisted censorship of the country, whereby certain issues can never be analyzed, let alone published as articles. In order to overcome some of these obstacles, Jack has become fluent in

Arabic, and he's thrown in his lot with the less well-off, socializing with youngsters labeled 'alternative,' and living with a local family in government-issued housing.

At the first rumblings, Jack decides to put his research on hold and to become a consultant for international organizations based in Tunis.

Jack says, 'Anonymous is my payback against censorship. It's also my revenge and my way of supporting these people who have hosted me and helped me, despite the impossible nature of my research.'

Jack is an IT buff. He is often connected to Anonymous and Operation Tunisia. This latter group is especially dynamic, creating and moving chat-rooms, and allowing thousands of cybernauts to use spaces that have yet to be closed down by censors. Thanks to IRC (internet relay chat) one of the earliest forms of instant messaging, Jack and other users can exchange information.

'It's an organic movement that surfs the web in continuous transformation,' Jack tells us with enthusiasm. 'And it's thanks to these chat-rooms that the request to attack government sites is broadcast. Software is distributed, allowing Anonymous to employ thousands of 'consenting' computers to carry through the DDOSA attacks (Distributed Denial of Service Account). All these machines connect simultaneously to the government sites, so they can no longer respond. As well as being effective, these attacks are symbolic, and demonstrate that the protest is now global.'

He continues, 'Most members of Anonymous hail from the United States, Europe and especially Northern Europe, where laws against hacking are not particularly rigorous. Very few of us are in Tunisia itself.'

Anonymous, to its benefit, is understood to be very influential. Having hitherto been criticized for hacking into various operations, it has the opportunity to improve its image by launching an attack against an unpopular government.

DEATH OF BOUAZIZI, BIRTH OF A MARTYR

We shall never forget you, Mohamed Bouazizi. We shall grieve for those who made you weep.
Slogan at Bouazizi's funeral

January 4th, Tunis, Ben Arous

After fighting for his life for many days, Mohamed Bouazizi dies on January 4th in the burns unit of Ben Arous Hospital of Tunis, from the third degree burns that cover 90% of his body. A crowd of 5,000 people takes part in his funeral, held in Sidi Bouzid. They chant in unison, 'Farewell, Mohamed; we shall avenge your death. Today we cry for you; tomorrow we shall make those who pushed you to your death cry.'

And along with the anger of the crowd, there is the courage of Mohamed's mother, who declares, 'I've lost my son, but I take pride in his achievement.'

Despite the large number of police preventing the mourners from reaching the square where Bouazizi self-immolated, nobody can stop the video of his funeral being viewed around the world. More than 70,000 viewers click onto YouTube, and so Mohamed's funeral is followed by a virtual community that doesn't hesitate to express its solidarity.

From Algeria, people comment, 'Bouazizi is our martyr. Allah himself will welcome you to Heaven. Your Algerian brothers will ponder this in their hearts. Bouazizi has demonstrated a life lesson.'

'He will be recorded in history as a symbol of the fight for justice, for reforms, for human rights and for freedom. People of the future will remember him and the reformation that will follow his death. Despite the sadness, we salute the honor of his sacrifice. The death of this man has offered hope for new life, and a fresh vision for everyone else. For this he will be memorable,' write people from the USA.

People from Iran post, 'God bless his soul. Rest in Peace, brother.'

Someone else comments, 'There will be more heroes like him.'

And in less than a month, this prediction comes true. Across a host of Arab countries, more people follow in Mohamed's footsteps. His death becomes the symbol of a betrayed generation, an icon in the fight against repressive regimes. Many supporters dedicate space to the movement both in print and on Facebook. The page, called Thank you, Mohamed, amasses thousands of fans from all around the world in a short time.

'This man is a hero for all populations in search of freedom,' affirms Dijali Beloufa from France. 'It's better to die as a hero than live as a coward,' writes Nigerian Obijaku Okey Herbert, a few days later. 'What has happened in Tunisia should be a warning to all other African leaders.'

Only a month after Mohamed's sacrifice, by which time his face is being printed on paper money, people are clamoring to have streets renamed in his memory, and more than 10,000 people have signed petitions to have many squares in Tunis renamed Bouazizi Square, instead of 'November 7th' (a reference to the date Ben Ali seized power).

Bertrand Delanoë, the Tunisian-born Mayor of Paris and member of the Human Rights League, dedicates a Parisian square in memory of the Tunisian martyr. The significance of Mohamed's sacrifice is summarized in a press release published by Attariq Al Jadid, a newspaper aligned with the Tunisian Communist Party, in which the death is described as an 'accusatory suicide.'

Latifa Lakhdar writes, 'only those who live in the shade of these obscene politics can describe such a suicide as trivial. It is an adversarial action, and the demonstrations triggered by it prove very clearly and incontrovertibly the validity of the accusation. It's a suicide that points the finger to the man and the regional institutions operating like strangers – or, worse enemies – instead of representatives of their own society. A citizen claiming a legitimate service is shown a cold shoulder by the authorities. Institutions not only neglect human and civil rights, but they consistently remind citizens of their bureaucratic and authoritarian entity, repeatedly demonstrating how far superior they are to everyone else.'

Analyzing Mohamed's death in more depth, it is pointed out that his true crime was to have believed in the ideal of citizenship. 'Unfortunately, the government and political parties per se are no longer capable of meeting society's needs, and in consequence are incapable of operating normally on a democratic level,' one person writes. And, finally, 'this suicide is an accusation against the deep-rooted corruption that is the basis of this government's modus operandi. It's an accusation against our false state of freedom and [quoting Seneca] 'the final act of a free man.''

Although self-immolation is prohibited in Islam, Mohamed's action is positively reinterpreted by believers as a sacrifice and not a suicide. Even Youssef al-Qaradawi, a very influential Sunni preacher based in the Magreb, justifies his action by asking one billion Muslims to pray to Allah for mercy, 'because his sacrifice has triggered the anger of a population to rebel against those leaders who work and live in sin.'

The first self-immolations to be used in this way took place in Vietnam during the 1960s, when Buddhist monks protested against South Vietnam's Ngo Dinh Diem regime. A few years later, a Czech student, Jan Palach, set himself on fire to protest the Red Army's invasion of Prague.

A few days after Mohamed's death, a new version of the events of that day starts to circulate. In this apocryphal version, Mohamed refused to hand over his scales to the policewoman, Faida Hamdy, replying, 'How am I supposed to weigh my goods? With your breasts, maybe?'

And that it was in response to this insulting remark that Faida started slapping and kicking Mohamed. The rest of the tale being circulated is basically the unadorned truth.

At this stage in the events, the policewoman is awaiting her trial; a clever plan intended to keep her from being lynched by an angry mob. In truth, the version told to the judges is irrelevant – what matters is that nothing can change the fundamental meaning of Mohamed's action and his position in Tunisian history as the first martyr of the revolution.

THE ROUNDUP OF BLOGGERS

The best jihad is saying the truth in the face of a dictator.

Arab Proverb

January 6th, Tunis

Slim Amamou, the director of a small IT company and a popular blogger, is arrested. He is not new to the police. A year ago he was jailed for having organized a protest against censorship. Following several hours of intensive questioning, he was forced to record and broadcast a video asking that the protest be cancelled. He was only then released. Relentless, Slim was not intimidated and continued with his work of criticizing the authorities, and following Mohamed's death, he didn't hesitate to point an accusatory finger.

'Mohamed's death has shaken us all,' he writes on a blog. 'I have seen a video recorded by a young man in Sidi Bouzid who witnessed what happened; I'm shocked to observe how little coverage these events have had in the media. I feel compelled to break this silence, and I and a group of friends are launching a new fight: events have happened so quickly that even the censors can't keep up with the rapidity of the information flow.'

A heavy Twitter user, at 1.00 pm on January 6th 2011, he sends his last tweet messages. The vast number of friends and colleagues in the habit of hearing regularly from Slim via Twitter lose track of his whereabouts. Some of his closest friends also realize that Slim will not answer the phone.

It is not until 6.00 pm that Slim's location can be ascertained. Through the social networking site FourSquare, which enables his detection by way of a geo-location instrument, they learn that Slim's cell phone is at this precise moment in the office of the Minister of the Interior, on Bourguiba Avenue.

An appeal for his liberation is simultaneously launched on Facebook and a vast number of blogs and IT platforms. Slim's popularity on and off the web soars accordingly.

Even so, not everyone agrees with the amount of attention accorded him. On one Facebook page devoted to his liberation, Emna writes, 'Slim Amamou's freeing is not my battle. There are so many more deserving people in prison; I don't want to be part of this group.'

Slim Amamou is not the only person to be arrested during this raid. Among the others are Slaheddine Kchouk (a militant student and blogger), Wael Naouar (a militant student), Ganja Tak (an activist blogger) Azyz Amamy (also an activist blogger), Hamadi Kaloutcha (a blogger and illustrator) and Wissem Sghaier (a journalist). Their names appear one after another on Facebook and Twitter as fellow bloggers trace who last saw them. And among them is the very popular young rapper, 'El General', who has been arrested because of the subversive content of his songs.

Slim and the others arrested are subjected to psychological torture.

Slim recounts, 'We were under all sorts of pressure. I was told that my friends and family were being tortured and raped in a room a few meters away from where I was being held. I was told that it had been necessary to call a doctor subsequently, and they left my door slightly ajar so that I could see a white-coated person carrying a bag pass by. I couldn't take it anymore, but I was aware of my human rights, as well as the cause I was embracing. I've been among the luckiest, thanks to the work of the movement for our liberation, and how it accelerated.'

News of the raid reaches the foreign press and is widely publicized, especially in French newspapers.

The anonymous cartoonist, Z, writes in his blog, 'Today more than ever, I'm convinced that this protest wasn't ignited by Mohamed Bouazizi, but by Ben Ali himself.'

THE COURAGE OF AN ABOUT-TO-BE MIGRANT

If you reach for the highest of ideals, you shouldn't settle for
less than the stars.
Arab Proverb

January 7th, Tripoli, Libya/Hammam Sousse

Hamza, age 29, has been unemployed for three months. He's a champion of handball, a popular sport in Tunisia, which he started to play when he was only seven. He's a strong, tall, muscular man, who reached the height of his success when selected to play for the national team for one year, after several years at club level with Club Africain. His inadequate salary of 160 Tunisian dinars (about $100 US dollars), and his little prize-money of 400 dinars from matches, are but small rewards for a man of Hamza's ability. He dreams of a normal life with a family and a more hopeful future. He's frustrated and disgusted by the corruption he witnesses in the world of sport, where the sons of ministers are allowed to play in the premier teams instead of much more capable players.

Once he finished doing his military service, Hamza found work on the margins of the tourist sector, hopping though various destinations of Tunisia's coast, initially working as a bouncer for night clubs, and then becoming head of security at a small hotel in Hammamet. He appeared to have achieved some stability in his life, but the hotel's owner was the protégé of one of Ben Ali's family members, and a highly-ranked friend. In serious debt, Hamza's employer stopped paying his employees. When they complained about the payment delay, their boss cited the burgeoning financial crisis and the risk of closing off the hotel. After this, and fearing for their jobs, nobody complained again until, in October of 2010, the hotel owner made good his escape to Switzerland. Then, Hamza's nightmare begins.

After months of looking for a new job he decides to go to Libya, with a plan to join the boatload of illegal migrants heading to Europe during the night.

On January 7th, however, just a few days before the departure, he receives a phone call from the National Guard, with whom he did his national service. They ask him to return to Tunis. The National Guard is looking for trustworthy people and he has been asked to join a volunteer force.

Back in Tunis, he's surprised by the change in his country. The atmosphere is tense and aggressive – the revolution has begun.

'I felt it was time for me to take part,' Hamza says. 'I'm not one who likes to parade down the street in protest, or to revolt against those in power. But being enlisted to defend my people is something that suits me better. And I have nothing to lose; if I'm shot, what will I lose?'

This demonstrates the despair and courage of people like Hamza, who have lost everything but can still see a way out – a change – and who want to be part of what is happening. When he joins the army, Hamza is transferred to Hammam Sousse, Ben Ali's hometown. He's asked to protect one of the president's palaces, but is given only a truncheon to fight against vandalism and the private militia.

Meanwhile, a number of articles emerge in Europe highlighting the deeper nature of the troubles in Tunisia. Domenico Quirico writes in Stampa, one of Italy'sleading newspapers that 'This is not a revolution yet, but it's more than a simple riot. It's a serious crisis, where the poverty of many is directly caused by the wealth of others'. In contrast to those who for years have praised Tunisia as 'the Switzerland of the Maghreb,' Domenico Quirico denounces this 'fake miracle'. 'The numbers are astonishing,' he writes. '87% of the population is literate, they have full health care and an annual revenue of 6,000 euro, an equal family law system and prisoners, especially those who are Islamists, who are very well looked after in jail. Thank you, Ben Ali! Of course, statistics can deceive. An economy based solely on tourism and the textile sectors is insufficient to provide jobs for young people, who are forced to attend high schools and university, in order to find jobs.' His description of the situation in Tunisia morphs into a prediction. 'It's a fake miracle, like the color of Ben Ali's locks. At the age of 64 he dyes and gels his hair black. The old, idolized leader has suddenly lost his teeth and made himself ridiculous in his obsession to retain his youth by any means. This lost generation has finally decided to delete him and to move on.'

THE WEST IS ASKED TO TAKE ACTION

History will have to record that the greatest tragedy of this period
of social transition was not the strident clamor of the bad people,
but the appalling silence of the good people.

Martin Luther King

January 8ᵗʰ, Rome

Tahar Ben Jelloun is a Moroccan writer who has lived in exile
in France since 1971. Back home, he was jailed for taking part in
student demonstrations. He was a popular figure in Maghreb. In
an open letter, he accuses France and Italy of being responsible
for the events unfolding in Tunisia and Algeria. His accusation
is that both countries have acted with condescension towards
regimes they know to be totalitarian. 'These are countries that
defeated terrorism by being victims of it originally,' he writes.
'Ben Ali's commitment to this matter cannot be ignored.'

To this, Franco Frattini, the Italian Minister of Foreign Affairs, replies, 'Riots are not caused by political issues, but by
global problems.' This comment encourages the press to label
the demonstrations, 'The Bread Riots.'

Gabriele Del Grande criticizes Frattini on his blog, 'We can't
accuse him of being incoherent; nor does the logic alter. The
lives of not everyone carry the same importance; and with this in
mind, it's perfectly acceptable to witness massacres in the Sea of
Lampedusa, or to watch young men and women being jailed in
Tripoli or in the Via Corelli, or to authorize a regime to open fire

on civilians in a square in the name of stability, which will always have a positive outcome, and in the name of anti-terrorism, which allows all countries to live permanently in a state of emergency security. Nonetheless, riots continue.'

Silvano, a research fellow in Islamic Studies at the University of Padova, says, 'This is not news emerging from the wild parts of Africa. It involves everyone directly, not only because of their geographic proximity, which is irrelevant in the global world, but because it's like seeing our own country in a crazy mirror. Tunisians and Algerians are reacting against the same economic and social injustices we are experiencing. Even so, middle-class Italians still view the rest of the world through crusades and religious wars, hiding behind the illusion that they are part of the civilized world where certain things just don't happen.' And he goes on to comment, 'Assange has already been forgotten, but the role played by the web, from the Middle East, to China, to our advanced democracies, cannot be forgotten.'

With the exception of a few countries, press coverage in the western world has been very limited. Journalist Francesca Bellino comments, 'At the end of the day, Italians have always looked at Tunisia as no more than a holiday resort. Consequently, they've only seen the smiling face of the nation, the evolving and prosperous image shown by the regime. They have no idea of what people, and especially youngsters, are going through. They've always been unable to initiate closer contact with the population, and at the same time the general populace has been unable to initiate conversation. Even journalists working for the major newspapers, and normally sensitive to the least signs of social change, have not taken the protests seriously. And they give the appearance of being surprised by a unique event not witnessed in the pages of recent history.'

Political analysts, diplomats and members of the opposition also accuse France of quietly supporting Ben Ali's regime. Some believe that Nicolas Sarkozi (the French president) and his administration have taken their eyes off the ball, to the extent that they are oblivious to recent events – and more so because for many years, they have enjoyed close relations with Ben Ali.

An opposition member of French parliament, Pierre Moscovici, comments, 'On the diplomatic front we're lacking in courage and dignity. I am ashamed of what I'm witnessing.'

TUNISIA'S 'BLOODY SUNDAY'

I can't believe the news today
Oh, I can't close my eyes and make it go away
How long, how long must we sing this song?
How long? How long?
U2 – Bloody Sunday

January 9th, Kasserine/Thala/Regueb

The day is a bitter awakening. Facebook pages are filled with images of the previous night's bloodshed. Monique posts a link accompanied by a U2 song, Bloody Sunday, written to remember the murder of Irish protestors by the British Army on January 30th 1972.

'The victims of the Tunisian Bloody Sunday amount to 50 in Thala, 22 in Kasserine, 2 in Meknassi, 1 in Feriana and 8 in Regueb. But this number increases in the course of the day, as police shoot into funeral processions.'

Jaouher, the father of a five-year-old girl, is the owner of a boulangerie in Kasserine. His story is similar to many others, in that he was forced to abandon his aspirations in view of little opportunity for advancement. Kasserine is a poor city in central Tunisia, not far from the Algerian border. It's underdeveloped and experiences a very high unemployment rate.

We interview Jaouher via Skype because we have no chance of getting to Kasserine. The interview can only be described as paradoxical. As an expert internet user, Jahouer takes us through the events of the day step by step, allowing us to 'enter' his computer and pointing out, using Google Earth, the places where demonstrations have taken place.

'As citizens of Kasserine, we're often mocked by fellow Tunisians who consider us peasants,' says Jaouher. 'It's almost impossible to marry a woman from outside Kasserine, because they're prejudiced against us.'

Having been forced by circumstance to abandon his studies, Jaouher decided to follow in his father's footsteps and become a baker. He now owns a shop in the center of the town, close to the police station. On Sunday morning, January 9th, he went for a short break to a café close to his shop, intent on fighting the extreme cold of the Kasserine winter with a warming drink. As he sat and watched, a funeral cortege of about two hundred people slowly proceeded past him. Suddenly, there came the noise of repeated gunshots.

'Policemen opened fire, but the procession didn't stop,' Jaouher tells us. 'The authorities tried to separate the men from the women, in order to aim at the men, but the crown bravely clung together. A few ran away, but others returned the gunfire with stones, the only weapons available. My mother begged me to stay where I was. She reminded me that I have a daughter to look after, but I just couldn't sit idly by.' That was not all. 'Later,' Jaouher continues, 'The police threw a tear gas canister outside a hammam (a Turkish bath) at the time it was the women's turn. Women ran out of the hammam half-naked, embarrassed and scared. And a six-month old baby girl died, after inhaling the gas. She was with her mother at the entrance to the hammam. All this – to entertain the police and humiliate our women!'

But the people of Kasserine do not give up.

'My son is dead, and my other three sons will die to avenge their brother's honor,' says one woman on Al Jazeera. A local blog is launched to inform everyone about Kasserine's genocide and the number of victims. Details about the first victims are speedily recorded. They gather evidence relating to the first underage victim, a youth of 16 killed at the door of his house in front of his parents' eyes, and also on a house painter shot in the back while he worked.

One citizen on the blog comments, 'This event symbolizes the misery of Kasserine. The government does not function, nor are we offered any way out. People do their best to survive, and instead they are killed on their doorsteps.'

The third death is of a 12-year-old boy, killed as he was standing beside his older brother. 'We have been sent here to invade this hell-hole,' boasts one of Ben Ali's special guards proudly to the father of the dead child.

'It's later in the afternoon, and snipers are positioned on the roof of the pharmacy,' says Ali, aged 18, to journalists. 'I'm standing at the corner of the street when suddenly I see my friend fall. I thought he'd tripped over something, but then I see blood pouring out of his smashed head. At that moment I notice a woman on top of the roof. It's her who shot him. She took out his brains as though she was just happy to hit a target.'

'General Ammar, Chief of the Army General Staff, was sacked last night for refusing to open-fire on the crowd,' comments Marzouki, a political opponent exiled to France. 'He has been replaced by another general, who is seen to be more malleable. If the army starts to shoot, it will be a massacre.'

It's the evening of January 9th. Houeida posts a message on Facebook that is simultaneously harsh and encouraging. 'Maybe the next step will be martial law – but at present it seems that the regime is losing control. More victims lead to more funerals, and more funerals lead to more protests. And shutting students out of school without even recourse to Facebook to keep them entertained is a recipe for disaster.'

With the help of doctors and nurses, videos taken in hospitals appear on the web – a vivid testimonial of the bloodshed. It would appear to be the point of no return.

According to Soufien, one of the bloggers who was arrested in the January 6th raid, 'The pivotal point is the images broadcast from the Kasserine morgue, especially the photos of a boy whose head was opened by a bullet through the back of his neck.'

On the internet, the watchword is to pin down the police in every city and prevent the dispatch of reinforcements to Kasserine, bringing an end to the massacres.

It is known that police have encircled the city, blocking access and exit to outsiders, particularly activists and bloggers like Lina Ben Mhenni. She's well-known to the authorities within the country and also to the international media. Lina is a young teacher of linguistics at the University of Tunis, and the daughter of a member of the Tunisian opposition. She's surprising in every way; very petite and very shy. Nobody meeting her would in their wildest dreams imagine that she's one of the bravest and most active voices opposing Ben Ali's regime. Her blog, A Tunisian Girl, is in written in English, and forges valuable connections during this time. 'My blog is my only lifeline' Lina tells us.

For more than two years Lina has in fact been threatened and shadowed, but never arrested. Being in contact with journalists worldwide gives her a certain, if fragile protection. Should she be arrested or just disappear, sufficient uproar from international media would trigger universal protests, especially from outlets such as France 24.

Lina is eager to share what is happening in Kasserine with the rest of the world, and anxious to show support for those who have taken up the fight for freedom.

Lina tells us, 'I grabbed my laptop and cell phone and jumped in my car, intending to drive to Kasserine. I knew very few people there, but nor did I need to. People have come to know me through my blog and the internet.' In truth, her whereabouts are often heralded through Facebook.

When she reaches Kasserine, her way is blocked by the National Guard.

One soldier addresses her by name, saying, 'Lina, I can't allow you in here. Please return to Sidi Bouzid.'

Lina receives a message from the city of Regueb, informing her that there has been bloodshed in Regueb as well. She decides to drive south, and by the evening she is within the bounds of the city. She drives directly to the hospital, which appears to be unguarded. However, there is no confusing the expression on the face of the emergency doctor. It reflects the horror of earlier hours, when victims of the massacre at Regueb arrived at the hospital. The shock can still be read on his face, and he's obviously scared. He would like to share what he has witnessed with Lina, but fear holds him back. It's not until he has locked himself into a small room with her that he lets himself unwind. He produces the medical records of the people who have been wounded and then subsequently transferred to the larger regional hospital. Lina listens and records everything. Then she goes to talk to the families of the victims, and before the night is done, she has published her findings on her blog.

'In that moment,' she records, 'I stopped thinking about my own fears. Nor did I want to censor myself in any way, or select my words with too much care. I felt I had to do something to honor the memories of all those people.'

Her first post, in English, reads, 'Five people were killed in Regueb: Manel Boallagui (26 years old) the mother of two small children, Raouf Kaddoussi (26), Mohamed Jabli Ben Ali (19), Moadh Ben Amor Khlifi (20), Nizar Bin Ibrahim (22). I shall give you more details later. In the meanwhile, I'll let the pictures do the talking. The images attached need no explanation; a distraught mother crying over the body of her son, an ambulance, the mess on the road following the demonstration.' Immediately, her blog is inundated with encouraging replies. One, from an anonymous blogger, but typical of the many she receives, reads, 'We're so proud of you, but at the same time we're frustrated that we're unable to help.'

Meanwhile, Ben Ali decides to address the nation again. He denounces the acts of terror perpetuated by 'rogues' who have been hired by foreigners, and sold their souls to extremists and terrorists.

Disappointingly, few responses on the recent events come from abroad; clearly, there is still tacit support for the current regime.

The number of victims increases through the day, but because of local censorship that has a hold over Facebook, the only source of information is Al Jazeera. It continues to broadcast details, despite some of its journalists being arrested. In the evening, a program is broadcast on the French channel

TV5, dedicated to following a group of youngsters calling themselves Mouvement Byrsa. Selim Ben Hassen, a young Tunisian living in France, asks how he can join the group. Within hours, the government has decided to close all the schools, on the pretext that they fear for the students' safety.

PROTEST REACHES THE UNIVERSITIES

My word is free. I am the red rose.
Amel Mathlouthi

January 10ᵗʰ, Tunis

Most lectures at the university have resumed, although discussion of politics are forbidden.

Twenty-one-year-old Mohamed explains, 'The universities are filled with spies. University police do little, apart from recording the names of those students considered to be dangerous, and hiring others to spy on in exchange for a few dinars. In public, nobody speaks about the current situation, everyone mistrusts everyone, even one's friends and neighbors could be spies recruited by Ben Ali. Students are under constant fear to be questioned or even kidnapped. So, they grow up fearful of becoming socially involved; they study, they go out at night – without ever talking about politics. From the time of high school they learn the complicated story of the royal family, including tales of this or that relative of Leila Trabelsi, who has seized control of a certain firm, or grabbed somebody else's land. Everybody knows what is happening, but nobody does anything about it.'

But on January 10ᵗʰ, enough people are prepared to make a stand. The students ready are primarily those whose university courses take place outside the capital and in other large cities, and who returned home for their vacations a few days before Mohamed Bouazizi's immolation.

Giorgioguido Messina writes on his blog, 'returning home to Sidi Bouzid, to Kasserine, to La Kef, students heard, for the first time, about the protests; and they could share with the protagonist's details that no radio station or TV channel would be privy to. Real truths: real facts.'

'When I returned to the university after three weeks of vacation, it all looked different. Tables have been spread out on the playground, and wherever I look, students are hard at work with paint, paper, cardboard and scissors. They are preparing posters supporting the revolution's martyrs, posters condemning censorship,' recalls Ameni Fakhet, a student at the Senior Institute of Fine Arts of Tunisia, and originally from Gabes, in the south. 'They're preparing slogans in Arabic, English, French, Italian and Spanish. In their anger and their desire to speak freely, the student body of Tunisia is communicating with the world. I'm witnessing scenes that have never before been seen. I join them in their work,' she continues.

Some of the students prepare and stage satirical shows about the president and his wife, and also about craven journalists. They are uncensored and hilarious. For the first time, the students are experiencing a censor-free environment. Then, spontaneously, someone suggests that they move out onto Avenue Bourguiba, in order to let the world know of their frustration and anger. It is then that they discover the police have surrounded the institute and closed the main entrance. The students do their best to force the door open, and for nearly an hour the opposing forces struggle as some of the students attempt to negotiate with the resolute police.

Some, who feel trapped, start to cry. Others, who are subsequently exposed to be members of the RCD Students' Wing, throw stones at the police, trying to provoke them.

The leaders of the students quickly shout, 'Stop! We are peaceful, and so is our action.'

Meanwhile, police back-up forces arrive, and they start to use their truncheons with force. Unarmed as they are, the students quickly retreat and are herded back inside the institute, where the crowd quickly dissolves. Although many of them are furious, they realize that victory must be delayed for another day.

This blood-spattered day is not, however, entirely in vain. It attracts the attention of the Italian media. While ANSA (an Italian news agency) gives the event brief coverage, Renato Caprile writes, 'Tunisia has reached a point of no return.'

Then, thanks to Catherine Ashton, Europe breaks its silence. She is the senior representative of EU Foreign Policy, and she roundly condemns the episodes of violence she has seen reported over the previous few days, demanding the immediate release of all dissidents who have been jailed. She reminds the government of the strength of the relationship between Tunisia and the EU, which is based on respect for human rights and fundamental freedoms.

That evening, a shocking video is broadcast, showing the entry of Ben Ali's Special Forces into Kasserine. Troops are seen breaking into houses and raping young women in front of their distraught parents. A male voice reports, 'They would knock on the door, and if there was no reply, they'd enter forcibly, beating the men and raping the women living there.'

Similar stories break out over the next few hours, from places as different as Tunis and Thala.

THE ARTIST'S DEMONSTRATION

One does not arrest Voltaire.

Charles de Gaulle

January 11th, Tunis/Kasserine

The main street of Kasserine is filled with the debris left behind from the previous day's riots, including the charred remains of buildings that have been torched. Journalists who have come to interview witnesses record the stories of those prepared to speak out. One person reports that while the police were shooting, people were cowering behind the army trucks. 'They were coastal police who were shooting,' says Ahmed. 'Not the army. Soldiers are different; they're okay. They've been born under the same sky as us.'

(The difference between the police and the army epitomizes the history of the Tunisian Revolution.)

'But the pivotal point was when we met the lawyers,' says Luciana Borsatti, a journalist from ANSA. 'Some of them wore their robes, as they followed the funeral processions of the most recent of Kasserine's victims. The funerals can be described as orderly and composed, even though the invocations to Allah sounded like slogans of protest.'

It is hard to deny that the lawyers represent the most lucid and militant aspects of the movement, which started from the heart of the country and is now reaching Tunis.

'Ordinary citizens have been mowed down by the police,' says Salma Abbasi, who has been a lawyer for twenty years. 'I saw the police fire directly on unarmed people. And what we're wondering now is who authorized the police to shoot, and then issued the order for them to pull out? They were here all of yesterday, and then suddenly they disappeared. Who gave the order for them to leave?' she repeats.

Meanwhile a group of artists, determined to support the protests of the last three weeks, makes the decision to gather in front of the Tunis City Theatre on Avenue Bourguiba. The demonstration is planned for noon, at which point actors, producers, musicians and painters start to gather on the sidewalk. A public disapproval of violence, they take their stand against the uncontrolled use of weapons by the authorities. Among their numbers are Daoudi Raja Amari and Jalila Baccar, two famous names in Tunisian theatre and cinema.

The group is quickly encircled by about a hundred police officers, who jeer, insult and jostle them around. The situation quickly escalates.

One of the artists within the group is Mourad, a film producer who studied and worked in Italy, and who still collaborates with Al Jazeera. Most of his work has been done abroad, where he's won many awards, and his sole contribution in Tunisia is one short film. Mourad lives in an apartment on Avenue Bourguiba, a few hundred meters from the theatre.

On January 11th, he decides to join the group of demonstrators. As soon as he enters the crowd gathering in Avenue Bourguiba, he sees Raja Ben Ammar, a well-known Tunisian actress, being verbally abused, hit, then pushed to the ground and having her hair pulled by a policeman. Mourad pushes his way through the group to go and be by the felled woman's side, managing to grab her by the hand. Her face is contorted with fear.

'I'll take charge of her. You can continue with someone else,' he says brusquely to the policeman. It's obvious that this disconcerts the him, and he's unsure how to proceed. Clearly, he recognizes Mourad, and perhaps it's this recognition that changes his mind. He moves on to jostling other members of the group.

The police continue with their confrontational behavior. Truncheons are in use, there's a lot of shouting and aggression. Then they start to herd the crowd towards a side street, at which point the artists are able to disperse.

Artists, as well as intellectuals, play an integral part in the mosaic of the Tunisian Revolution. In a scenario where freedom of expression is limited by means of force, they have still managed to purvey, directly and indirectly, an alternative political message and thus create small cracks in the system.

Mohamed Mediouini, director of the Higher Institute of Dramatic Arts, says, 'Even under Ben Ali's censorship, artists have repeatedly pushed the limits.'

Apart from a few small 'privileges' such as on occasion being able to join a company or two, most artists have suffered constant bullying over the course of many years. They have been unable to rent spaces for rehearsals, are expelled from contests, or even denied from accepting rewards.

'Over the years, both in the theater and in the cinema, we have witnessed different methods of opposition, ways to disagree with the conformism forced on us by the government. But in this last year the government has been promoting Ben Ali's candidacy for the upcoming elections, and this has triggered a psychological breaking point, especially among young people who can no longer see a future perspective. The number of suicides has increased dramatically, despite their remaining undocumented,' comments Mourad.

Some people decide to leave. This was the case of Ahmed Hafiene, a notorious Tunisian actor who has now lived in Europe for several years after escaping the restrictions of his country, 'where the culture doesn't represent the nation's needs, but is a shop window with nothing behind the window.' Married to an Italian journalist, Ahmed has enjoyed a successful life, and loves his new home in Rome, despite being a city, 'where Arabs are often regarded with a jaundiced eye'. Now, Ahmed is suffering. He would like to support Mourad, his friend and best man at his marriage, but it's not possible. He can only follow events via Facebook and Radio Kalima. He appreciates that this protest is different from previous attempts, largely thanks to the efforts of young people hitherto excluded by the rest of the world, and now able to access news from home via their computers. And, moreover, since they have found the courage to initiate a protest even without the need of a leader.

Simultaneously, hundreds of Tunisians respond to an appeal from the doctors for blood donations. They gather at Geant, the country's biggest shopping center, where blood collection points are set up. A video appears on the web, and the message is strong and clear. This time around, the people are united, and they are no longer afraid.

THE REVOLUTION REACHES HAMMAMENT; AND THE WORLD WAKES UP

If you are strong...
Rescue me from this ocean
For I don't know how to swim
Nizar Qabbani, Message From Underwater

January 12th, Hammamet

Hammamet, along with Djerba, is one of the most popular tourist resorts - favored by European travel agencies as a 'last-minute' destination. Its white beaches and crystal-clear water attract hundreds of Germans seeking to escape the seasonal cold of their country.

The wave of demonstrations reaches Hammamet unannounced.

Aldiana runs a chain of hotels noted for their perfect organization and excellent cuisine, although frequently criticized for the inflexibility of their concierges. What very few people know is that Aldiana is owned by Belhassen Trabelsi, the brother of Ben Ali's wife.

It is just after noon. Zouhair Souissi, husband of Farah Ben Hammoud and a concierge at the 5-star hotel Wella Azu, finishes work in Nabeul.

A demonstration is taking place, and Zouhair is anxious to get back to Hammamet. Small groups of protestors have taken to the streets, and others are joining them. Simultaneously, Farah arrives at her mother-in-law's house. Once there, she calls her eldest son, imploring him not to join the demonstrators.

At 3.00 pm, she receives a call from her husband. He is about to leave for home but wants to detour to discover what is going on. He is, of course, still in his work uniform. By the time he reaches the demonstration, the protestors have reached the police station, and the situation is chaotic. Assorted people mingle with the crowd, although Zouhair is only aware of one person dressed in black. Wanting to contact his wife, Zouhair moves away from the crowd and takes out his cell phone. He is about to speak when gunshot is fired. Zouhair collapses onto the pavement, covered in blood. Nobody can point a finger at the shooter - it might have been a sniper, it might not.

Farah is contacted immediately, as Zouhair is quickly taken to the nearest clinic. Sadly, it is not equipped to handle such emergencies, and so Zouhair is rushed to the central hospital. He dies ten minutes later from severe hemorrhaging. He is one of several patients there being treated for gunshot wounds.

To add insult to injury, the hospital authorities refuse to return the body, saying that Zouhair was an opponent of the state. The administration wants his family to sign a declaration not mentioning the cause of his death. Outraged, they refuse to sign. So negotiations begin, and it's not until some days later that the body of Hammamet's first martyr is buried. Unfortunately, he is not alone. Immediately after the shooting of Zouhair, a second person is murdered.

A few weeks after her husband's death, Farah contacts a lawyer specializing in human rights. Her one hope is to discover who was responsible for his death. Today, she is still no closer to finding the killer.

Meanwhile, a few kilometers from Hammamet, Sihem Ben Hadj Alaya is terrified.

'There's chaos in the street,' she says. 'When I peek out of the window, I see people everywhere trying to find refuge. I quickly close the window, fearing for the safety of my children. Suddenly, a group of young people bursts into my house. They're carrying a boy with a great, gaping wound on his right leg. He's in awful pain, and I find myself shivering with fear. However, I pull myself together and do my best to help him. I can offer him the limited choice of painkillers that I have available, cover his wound and make him as comfortable as possible. Outside the sound of gunshots echoes and reverberates. There are pounding feet, as the police chase the demonstrators. A few minutes later a car draws up, and people run in to gather up the wounded boy and take him to the hospital. Some of the demonstrators accompany the boy, others mingle with the crowd. As suddenly as it was invaded, my house is empty. I turn to my children. I've watched them do their best to comfort and help the wounded lad. They did so with pride and honor and absolutely no fear. I'm so proud of them.'

On the same day, Monique broadcasts a video entitled, The Media is With Us. It contains an extract from the news, a report on the police attack of a television troupe filming the scene. The images and the message it conveys are clear, and overcome the language barrier. Later, witnesses report that the journalists were not directly attacked by the police, but swept along by the crowd. The video has an explosive impact, affording hope to all Tunisians – they have at last caught the attention of the international press. It has been a long time coming.

That day, Ben Ali announces, through Prime Minister Ghan-nouchi, that the Minister of Internal Affairs, Rafik Kacem, has been dismissed. He's been accused of ordering the police to fire on the demonstrators. A judicial enquiry against corruption is simultaneously launched, alongside the freeing of those people arrested since the start of the protests. The statement has all the hallmarks of an attempt to placate the protestors. It fails.

The government declares a curfew for all of Tunis. People are barred from leaving their houses between 8.00 pm and 5.00 am. The curfew has evidently been proposed with the intention of protecting citizens from the incidents, ravages and violence that have occurred in certain neighborhoods.

And finally, that evening the European Parliament threatens to break off negotiations between Tunisia and the EU.

THE DOWNFALL

> *Think! Whenever you reap*
> *the heads of men and the flowers of hope,*
> *wherever you water the heart of the earth with blood*
> *and inebriate it with tears,*
> *the flood will carry you away, the torrent of blood,*
> *and the burning rage will consume you.*
> Abou el Kacem Chebbi, To the Tyrants of the World

January 13ʳᵈ, Tunis/La Marsa

'This has been a night of gunshots in many neighborhoods,' comments one of the doctors in the emergency department of Rabta Hospital in Tunis. 'It's been the worst experience of my life. I've seen many innocent people dying. They've been killed by police fire. One after another has passed away.'

Dr. Mzah adds, 'It's a massacre. There are people with crippling injuries, three people killed and many young people badly hurt. I'm filled with fury when I think of this manhunt; some victims were chased and shot down on their own doorsteps. A child arrived at Ben Arous Hospital carrying another child, who had been shot through the heart.'

From the emergency room, Mahmoud writes, 'I saw a 17-year-old boy with a bullet in the left hip and a compound fracture. The police had beaten him like a dog, then thrown him in a toilet and urinated on him.'

Tunisians respond with courage to this appalling abuse of power. Olfa, a young teacher, launches an appeal to create a group who will help to repair the damage; tidying, fixing and rebuilding houses, shops and streets. She says, 'When the government imposed a curfew on January 12th, and while we were still hiding in our homes feeling angry and powerless, some people went out deliberately to ransack and destroy shops and streets. Why didn't the police and the army, who are supposed to protect us, intervene? Tunisians aren't terrorists. Looters are a small minority; they don't represent the population of Tunisia.'

Using his blog, Gabriele Del Grande publishes a collection of horrifying videos[29]. 'These images convey a very powerful message,' he writes. 'They are the videos of the martyrs; young men who elected to fight and paid with their lives. They were killed by the police, who have been sent by Ben Ali with orders to shoot on sight.'

Although under the January sun, Tunis is seemingly tranquil, the atmosphere remains tense. We go to work and everything appears normal until 10.00 am, when we receive a phone call from our friend, Saoussen, informing us that there will be another demonstration, and possibly a riot. It would be wise to close our office by noon. Even the watchman of our building knows this – apparently everyone in the neighborhood has been informed.

At 12.00 pm, we see the truth in all this. Many shops have shut, and people make for home at a quick rate. We descend in the elevator and run to our parked car. The entrance of the park-

---

29 http://fortesseurope.blogspot.com/2011/01/martiri.html

ing lot, only a couple of meters from the exit, is closed. The watchman opens it as he sees us. We jump into the car and make rapidly for home.

Pierrick Ancel, a young French artist living in Tunis, is at the French Institute of Cooperation in the town center.

He recalls how, 'In the early afternoon the atmosphere seems tranquil. Suddenly, I hear the sound of gunshots, right outside the building. I glance at my colleagues to note their reactions. Then, an hour later, when things appear to be calmer, I go out onto the balcony to have a smoke. The noise is getting closer; people start wondering aloud how they might reach their homes. Meanwhile they look at me, remarking on how I can stay so calm and immersed in my drawings. Am I an artist or vampire? I carry on with my work. Below, on the street, people are running, screaming and throwing things. Then the police start shooting again. The fight is brutal. In this creative restlessness, I scribble feverishly. Then, the director of the institute enters, telling me to evacuate the building and apologizing for asking me to come to work. But leaving is not so easy. Evacuation will mean everyone ending up on the street, in the middle of the riot. As it happens, the security people let us out via the back door. Teargas canisters have been thrown and people are walking fast with scarves around their faces to avoid inhaling the gas. Men, women and children all stream in the same direction. We can hear explosions, but this time they sound further away. There are no cars on the road, and almost all the stores are closed. Trams and buses have ceased to run and all the taxis seem to be full. The drivers of some cars are offering to give people lifts.'

In the evening, Ben Ali plays his trump card; for the first time in his 23 years in power, he delivers a speech in Tunisian-Arabic.

In using a different tone this time around, he makes a last-ditch attempt to reach out to his people. He condemns the use of weapons and promises to catch and punish those responsible. He admits that he has made mistakes, blaming those around him who did not advise him properly, and who failed to inform him about the real state of the country. He promises freedom of the press and of expression, just as he promises democracy and free access to the web. He also promises to reduce the price of bread and flour, and finally announces that he won't stand for re-election in 2014. This last promise contrasts starkly with all of his earlier speeches.

He closes with a sentence that will forever remain written in the pages of Tunisian history: 'Fahim Tukum; I have understood you.' In saying this, he quotes General de Gaulle in Algeria on June 4th 1958, when, in trying to placate the Pieds-Noirs (the local French community), he led everyone to believe that he wished to keep Algeria under French control. His speech raised hope in every citizen, only for it to be dashed when Algerian independence was announced shortly afterwards.

His choice of words is not seen as accidental. It will be repeatedly quoted, and its intention questioned. A few weeks later an organization inspired by Ben Ali's words will be formed to create a platform for better understanding the government, and supporting the democratic movement[30].

The ban on YouTube is immediately lifted. 'Six hundred more people swell the unemployment list,' Wafa comments acidly, referring to the many who until now have worked on web

---

[30] www.fhimt.com

censorship, and have just become redundant. Earlier on, Wafa escaped from Tunisia to live in Barcelona.

Bousufi is a Tunisian who migrated to Italy. His blog is full of photos of the young people killed by the authorities in their attempts to quell the riots[31]. 'Have eighty of our brothers died just for this? Only to make YouTube visible or reduce the price of sugar by a cent?' he asks, then provides his own answer. 'No. They died to free their country, and to redeem their loved ones for a future without Ben Ali; a future no longer filled with lies and fear. Our companions have died for their fellow Tunisians all over the world. They have died to allow us a better future. I'm ashamed of myself for not having been there to fight alongside you; you who would have welcomed me with open arms, had I joined you.'

A few minutes after the president's speech, the sound of horns echoes through the neighborhood. How, we wonder, can people be ignoring the curfew and risking death, merely to celebrate a speech? It seems incomprehensible to us.

And many of the activists are troubled. 'If the people can be won over with only a few concessions,' comments Monique, 'the government will quickly revert to its old policies, and the lives of all of us who have risked so much will be endangered. In only a few months, people will forget all that has happened, and Ben Ali will have won again.' Her thoughts reflect the opinions of many people.

Similarly, Ahmed, the famous Tunisian actor, echoes Monique's sentiments on his Facebook page. 'If this is the end

---

[31] http://bousufi.blogspot.com

of the revolution, Ben Ali will pick off the demonstrators one by one.'

One or two brave souls venture out to identify the source of the honking. The videos they take, as well as the words of eye witnesses, verify that the din emanates from a number of hired cars – all of which have identical blue and white number plates and unidentifiable horns.

'It's a joke!' producer, Mourad exclaims. 'There is only one reason to celebrate – they all say, 'Ben Ali must go!' If you turn up at tomorrow's demonstration, we'll count how many slogans there are.'

News of the fake celebrations, no more than rental cars employed by Ben Ali's party, reaches Paris and is broadcast by France 24. 'It's a farce organized by Ben Ali's henchmen,' is their take on proceedings.

Once again, the quiet of the night is punctuated by the sound of shooting. How come? Didn't the president promise there would be no more violence?

The revolution has not ground to a halt. As the night wears on, messages and strong support fill websites and blogs. Support for the demonstrations increases exponentially.

DEGAGE (LEAVE)

Let the heavens roar with thunder
Let thunderbolts rain with fire.
Men and youth of Tunisia,
Rise up for her might and glory.
Tunisian National Anthem

January 14th, Carthage / Tunis

Olfa, who is 35, decided to join the RCD (Ben Ali's party) with the conviction that she might influence things from within. Today, she knows better.

The party has called an emergency meeting at its headquarters, which are situated not far from Avenue Bourguiba. It is, coincidentally, where thousands of Tunisians have gathered intending to initiate a general strike. The events of recent days have shaken Olfa; she has witnessed tourists fleeing and policemen striking people with their batons. She herself was forced to seek shelter for several hours behind the shutters of her father's travel agency. Then she'd made for home, to her daughters, ever fearful of being stopped en route.

'Our freedom has been jeopardized,' she says. 'I know that we can't carry on like this.' She makes up her mind to ignore the party's invitation to attend the emergency meeting, and informs the leaders that instead, she will be joining the protests the following morning.

Meanwhile, the situation in Carthage is one of unnatural calm. Few people go to work, and a chilly silence descends over the neighborhood. We all seem to be waiting for the culmination of the Tunisian Revolution, as the bloggers have started to label it.

Despite the president's attempts at pacifying the situation pacification, we have witnessed another heated night. Facebook is filled with messages inviting and exhorting people to show up at the city center, and offering lifts to those who might normally catch public transport. All these means of travel have been suspended. The atmosphere is tense.

Many expats are glued to their television sets and computer screens, waiting to hear news from family and friends. The police and the army have been mobilized to stand side by side. Tanks rumble along the streets on patrol.

'Tunisians can thank France for the gift of this jewel that has hosted Tunisian history for a century' comments Mohamed Kilani, succinctly describing Avenue Bourguiba[32], the elegant thoroughfare inspired by the Champs Élysées. Originally, Bourguiba (and subsequently Ben Ali) used the avenue for large-scale parades in front of excited crowds. As time has progressed, however, the crowds have become less effusive in their acclamation.

And now, on Friday, January 14th, this same avenue hosts the largest protest it has ever witnessed – this time against Ben Ali.

By lunchtime, the first videos are being flashed around the world. Thousands of people take part; estimations range be-

---

[32] M. Kilani, La Revolution des Braves, Impression Simpact, Tunis, 2011.

tween 5,000 and 50,000. Numbers may differ – but one fact is indisputable. This is a peaceful demonstration.

Monique has instructed her 15-year-old daughter to stay home for safety reasons. Now, she asks her ex-husband to bring the girl over to the avenue, in order to witness history in the making. 'Come along,' she shouts over her cell phone. 'There aren't any snipers about.'

Word of mouth is hugely influential. The crowd swells as similar messages fly about the town. The avenue becomes more and more packed, people feeling secure in the knowledge that they will be part of one huge gathering.

Asma, the 22-year-old law student, is there with her father, a Tunisian lawyer. They mingle with the crowd, her following a line of youngsters, and her father joining a group of fellow lawyers. By 2:00 pm, Avenue Bourguiba is packed.

A white van makes its way with difficulty through the densely-packed crowd. It's carrying the body of a boy killed the previous day.

Luciana Borsatti, the head of Tunisia's office of ANSA, reports, 'One lad is holding a bunch of flowers. The funeral has been organized by Helmi's friends. He was a 24-year-old student who lived in the Bab al Khadra neighborhood, and was killed by a sniper during one of the protests in the city center. His friends decided to have him join today's demonstration, before the actual funeral.'

Asma makes her contribution with the Zaghrid, which is a popular Arab celebratory whistle used by women. 'Allah Akbar!' (Allah the Great) shout the men. A second demonstration, which started at the headquarters of the main trade union, converges on Avenue Bourguiba, where people start calling for Ben Ali's departure, chanting 'Dégage, dégage' (go away).

'Suddenly I was left alone, as I lost my colleagues journalists,' recalls Luciana. I found comfort in the sigh of Sami, a government official standing by the demonstrators. His expression clearly showed his sympathy for the demonstrators. So, I decided to walk alongside him. We passed a police cordon without any problem and proceeded towards the city center. When we reached Avenue Bourguiba and saw the number of people there we were incredulous. Sami's eyes expressed his sincere belief that we were about to witness momentous change.'

A police blockade has been put in place in the hope of deterring the protesters. Along with the rest of the crowd, film producer Mourad sings heartily. He stares at the policemen who are dispersing the crowd and splitting the protesters into various groups. He starts marching far from the front lines, but quickly finds himself closer and closer to the police, joining the front row of the rally they are trying to break through. He ends up face-to-face to a young policeman. He is chanting the Tunisian national anthem. He bravely stares him in the eyes and for a few seconds, their gaze meets. It's just enough time to see tears dropping from the eyes of the young policeman. 'It's at this moment that I realized we can still make it,' he says. He pushes his way through the police, followed by the crowd. The second demonstration merges with the first. People mingle.

Somebody shouts, 'We can live with only bread and water, but we do not want Ben Ali.'

Victory is near.

The Tunisian Ambassador to UNESCO tends his resignation in protest of the increasingly repressive methods used in Tunisia.

At 4.15 pm, Ben Ali dismisses the entire government and announces that fresh elections will be held in six months. A state of emergency is declared.

Luciana Borsatti explains, 'This means that there will be a nationwide curfew, and a ban on more than three people gathering at any time. Police and the army are permitted to shoot at anyone disobeying these laws. Airspace has been shut down. Tunisians are, essentially, trapped.'

The regime has started to totter. Apparently, certain members of the Trabelsi family have tried to leave the country, but Mohamed Ben Kilani, a captain with Tunisair, the Tunisian national airline, makes a heroic gesture. He boldly refuses to allow members of the president's family to board the plane. 'I've done my bit, as a Tunisian,' he will declare later, 'And all the crew supported my decision. Denying them permission to board the plane has been my way to participate in the demonstration.' These people are later arrested.

Despite the airport being closed, Ben Ali manages to escape. Witnesses living in Sidi Bou Said see his family yacht leaving the port. Messages start to appear on the internet, questioning why it is that he can leave, while everyone else is held captive.

In the meantime, in Salemi, a small village in the heart of Sicily, (just a few hundred kilometers away from Tunisia) resides Lilia Zaouali, a Tunisian historian. She is nervously following recent events. All is quiet in this remote place, and she feels she is missing out on history in the making in her home country. Following events through Facebook makes her feel close to her fellow Tunisians.

While all her Italian friends seem to be unaware of the events happening in her home country, she receives a call from Paris.

'Lilia, he's gone! He's left!' It takes Lilia a few confused seconds to realize that it's Ben Ali who has left. 'Tunisia's free! It's all over, and at the same time it's all beginning.'

She is thrilled and excited, but she has no one around her with whom she can share her emotions. She turns around to her Italian friend, happy to pass on the news. 'Did you hear than Ben Ali is gone?' 'How would I know? I do not even know what is going on in Salemi.' he exclaims angrily.

Although it is only a few hundred kilometers away, Tunisia is living through a moment of historical significance, and the little strait of sea that divides Sicily (and Europe) from Tunisia seems an infinite ocean.

Soon though, the initial joy Lilia felt turns into concern for her family back home, in the Northern city of Bizerte, where unrest is intensifying and Ben Ali loyalists seem to be setting up fires in last attempt to create chaos.

At about 6.00 pm, an alert is posted on the web, warning of a potential coup d'état in Tunis. The mixture of speculation and actual fact makes knowing what is true almost impossible, and it will remain this way until a provisional government is announced.

Almost immediately, the news on Facebook is packed with messages spilling over with joy. Somebody has already changed the signature page, replacing the Tunisian flag with one colored black – as a symbol of solidarity with the people of Tunisia, and of mourning for the deaths of the those fallen during the revolt.

Finally, the people of Tunisia have won.

Snippets of news about the president's whereabouts seep in one by one. Some say that Ben Ali's private jet has landed in Italy, others in France. The Tunisian Embassy in Paris is surrounded by demonstrators, as is the French Embassy in Tunis. France finds itself under pressure, since the people of Tunisia react with greater speed than the French Ambassador. He is subsequently sacked after sending a statement to Paris informing the government that the situation is under control.

Tension throughout the country is high.

'For more than twenty years nothing has happened in Tunisia; then in less than twenty-four hours we have seen first a demonstration in the square acclaiming Ben Ali – followed by a demonstration today in which thousands of Tunisians demanded that he quit – thus by the declaration of a state of emergency – and the flight of the president.'

'The celebration by Ben Ali's fans might well have led to a temporary stability, but today's demonstration, along with the general strike, confirms that an unanticipated degree of freedom has finally arrived,' comments an ANSA journalist. 'Posters appear, the flags of Tunisia and Che Guevara are hoisted. Other demonstrations take place simultaneously in Kasserine, in Gafsa and Sid Bouzid, where everything started, although police charges shatter the dreams of many people, as they throw teargas canisters to make the crowd dissipate, and chase anyone still refusing to withdraw.'

At 9.00 pm, a message is posted on Facebook confirming that the big Carrefour superstore managed by one of Ben Ali's daughters has been burned down, the harbinger of another night of fire. Other messages advise people to take precautionary measures, criticizing the army for not managing to maintain control.

We hear repeated gunshots. We try to put the children to bed, but for the first time we're really jittery and scared. Through the open window we can smell burning and hear yet more gun-fire, along with discharging rifles. We decide that we must pre-pare for the worst-case scenario, so we lock all the doors, gather up some clothes and all our documents, (stacking them together and keeping them close at hand) just in case we should be forced to leave in a hurry.

Although the main targets appear to be shops owned by the president and his family, and not private properties, we also hear that apartment blocks and villas have been ransacked. This is always a secondary consequence of any revolution; opportunistic people take advantage of the state of confusion to loot.

The assumption that there's been a coup d'état by the army gains ground as it is reported more frequently on the blog-osphere and in several papers. This hypothesis is also supported by the Italian journalist Lorenzo Cremonesi of the Corriere della Sera[33], who thinks this will explain why General Ben Ammar re-fused to shoot at the crowd, and why many other officers have not taken part in the repression in recent days. In his view, they are planning to intervene at any moment.

Miriam, who has two small children, is home alone. Her hus-band, Antonello, works at the Italian Embassy. Today he's on duty, guarding the office and helping any Italians living in Tuni-sia. Miriam is too scared to sleep. Suddenly she hears noises coming from the street. A group of four or five men has entered her garden over the high wall. Her heart pounds more and more strongly as the noise they make increases. She calls her husband – the line is busy. With trembling fingers, she calls the ambassa-

---

[33] L. Cremonesi, I generali rimasti a guardare, I motori di un "golpe"mori-bondo, Corriere della Sera, 14 January 2011.

dor's line, and manages to reach him. 'Men are trying to break into my house!' she screams.

Finally, the embassy manages to alert the police. They arrive before the intruders have managed to break in. Just in time.

THE DAY AFTER

Avoid cruelty and injustice,
for on The Day of Judgment,
the same will return into several
darknesses.
Revolution Slogan

January 15th, Carthage/ Tunis/ La Marsa

The night appears to have been quieter than we might have expected. No medical bulletins have been released, and there have been no further demonstrations. Most people have respected the curfew. Only one disturbance is reported between the police and some hot-heads intent on vandalizing property and stealing from shopping centers. It is sometime later that we discover Ben Ali's Special Forces were involved. The sporadic looting of houses appears to be limited to the properties of the president and his family, and bears all the hallmarks of personal revenge. When daylight returns everything appears normal, people are wandering in the streets.

Mourad is on his way to Avenue Bourguiba, intending to meet friends for breakfast. They were unable to return home before curfew after yesterday's demonstration because they were deeply involved in discussing possible plans for the future, as well as their fears.

Ayoub Jaouadi, an actor and Mourad's guest, was arrested while on his way home. He was taken to the Ministry of the Interior, where he was mistreated for hours, interrogated and beaten, the intention being to make him reveal which foreign country he works for. This is a futile attempt to set a precedent and to establish proof of foreign intervention, in order to discredit the entire revolutionary movement. During the interrogation and beating, the police make it known that they have consistently followed every movement of Mourad and his friend since the previous evening.

Security in our own office is advising all the staff members to keep any movement to the minimum. The Monoprix supermarket in the expat neighborhood has been partly burned down and the windows smashed in, probably during the clashes between the police and vandals. Passers-by are availing themselves of the opportunity to loot the store, while others look on. Suddenly, two police cars arrive at top speed, shooting in the air as they go like cops in a western movie. Looters and onlookers alike take to their heels. Meanwhile, air and sea routes are partially reopened. Tunisair resumes its flights to and from Europe. The appearance of normality is, however, quickly shattered as groups of armed men take it upon themselves to guard neighborhoods and helicopters begin to patrol overhead. It seems that there's been a confrontation between the final dregs of Ben Ali's Special Units and the army. Warning messages are circulating on the web. 'Take care' one says, 'Should police knock at your door, don't open! Many of the police and special forces have deserted to join the looters.'

'I've just escaped from La Marsa,' Olfa posts on her Facebook wall. 'Militia and policemen with machine guns are everywhere. They're shooting indiscriminately. Trust the police no longer.'

Many expats put into motion their plans to leave the country.

The turning point comes in the afternoon, when the presidency passes from the prime minister to the parliamentary secretary, where it is intended to stay until new elections are held. This simple constitutional passage finally quenches the recent fears that power might be quietly transferred back to the party elite. In fact, Article 57 of the Constitution, introduced by Ben Ali himself, states that, should the president be temporarily unable to exert his role, power can be transferred to the prime minister, and then subsequently transferred back. Ben Ali's departure and and the transferral of power to the parliamentary secretary, who as it happens has also left the country, eliminates any hope that the RCD could return to power.

Meanwhile, groups of vigilantes continue to form. Young men armed with batons start to patrol the neighborhoods.

In Cairo, a demonstration has been organized in support of all Tunisians. Slogans read, 'Revolution today in Tunisia; tomorrow in Egypt!'

Tunisia is achieving a massive breakthrough; the possibility of similar revolutions spreading to other Arab countries is no longer a pipe dream.

Inshallah la bes (God willing, we are going to be fine).

THE BATTLES OF CARTHAGE AND THE BIRTH OF A NEW COUNTRY

Do not be afraid of what is hiding behind the hills.
It is just only the morning light.
Abou El Kacem Chebbi

January 16th, Carthage

It's daybreak and gunfire can be heard from our neighborhood. Even so, the web reports no acts of violence, and on the surface the situation appears tranquil. The security report from one international organization reads, 'Today looks like it will being calm. Staff members can leave their houses, but we suggest that you avoid long-distance travel'. Even so, we can still hear sporadic gunfire.

The first 'neighborhood watch' committees are created – the members, all civilians, are only armed with batons. These groups are formed in direct response to an earlier appeal from the army, broadcast over the radio and Facebook. Hisham Ben Khamsa writes, 'In order to help the authorities in their peaceful mission, we invite all Tunisians to form neighborhood vigilance committees, groups of five or six men armed with batons, rods or anything else, patrolling a maximum of three or four blocks. We need group leaders who can stay in contact with similar committees close by. Guard duties should not exceed two or three hours, so that everyone may have a chance to rest. Once curfew is over, it would be appreciated if you could offer any authorities resting close to you hot beverages and food. Please spread the word'.

Side roads are blocked by rudimentary barriers made of cactus, wooden beams, stones and other tools. 'They walk up and down with their batons and cell phones, videoing each other,' comments one Facebook user, offering a moment of levity to other users. Among this group of guardians immortalized through the web is the funny ex-official photographer of the Ministry of Tourism, who happens to have a particularly long mustache, and also the chatterbox owner of a DVD shop, who, as well as loving the sound of his own voice, is bald and fat.

But after these minutes of lightened atmosphere, the gunfights resume. They seem to be more frequent and getting closer.

How can we make sense of all this to children of two and four?

'Kids,' we might say. 'Your Playmobile army is real.'

We joke about what is happening while trying to work out the solution to this problem. Then the children make up their own game, creating bad people on the run with the police in hot pursuit, chasing and capturing them. It's a bit too close to the reality of the situation for comfort – a game reflecting all that's transpired on the streets and in the squares of the city in recent weeks, in which policemen switch from protectors to aggressors when they murder and maim fellow citizens, and in which the army defies orders and refuses to attack the crowds, morphing into the only force capable of restoring order. It's a game in which hitherto law-abiding and peaceful citizen demonstrators join criminals to loot and steal, becoming occasional burglars and merciless avengers. Moreover, in this game, some policemen join the burglars to rob, while the 'beagle boys' do their best to establish a degree of order in the neighborhoods.

It's a game of parts, which is of course the problem. To our children, this very unpredictability gives rise to enjoyment.

While battle rages in Carthage, other news filters through; international flights have resumed, and many employees of large companies are being repatriated.

Luciana Borsatti says, 'The civilians in Tunisia are trying to hang in there. They're defending themselves from armed gangs ravaging the country, shooting and robbing. Institutions are doing their best to save the country, particularly in respect to the constitution, by way of a broad, coalition government, and knowing how little time is available – and despite this being the only political response to the profound crisis the country is experiencing. So, too, is the movement created subsequent to Mohamed's sacrifice in Sidi Bouzid trying to hang in there. It's a movement originally formed to denounce the despair of so many unemployed, that has quickly become a movement to support freedom, the dignity of a nation and, most of all, the end of a dictatorship.'[34]

More information is broadcast on the web. The army is not looking for common criminals, but for 1,000 (others report 3,000) soldiers employed in Ben Ali's Special Forces, who were released only a few hours after the arrest of Ali Seriati, head of Ben Ali's security. Seriati played a key role in the Special Forces and in managing government television channels. He has been accused by many information sites of plotting against the new

---

[34] L. Borsatti, Si cerca la svolta politica: battaglia a Cartagine, ANSA, 17 January 2011.

government structure, of spreading terror via gunfights, and of acts of burglary and violence.

ANSA reports similarly, 'Clashes between Ben Ali's faithful militia and the authorities supporting the current institution have resulted in hours of gunfire centered around the Ministry of Interiors and the Hotel Africa, where the international press is quartered. The hotel's entrance doors have been reinforced with metallic barriers, and are patrolled by plainclothes police. This hotel houses tens of journalists, who report the news live to a background of gunshots, low-flying helicopters and the sounds of car chases in a deserted and lifeless Avenue Bourguiba. Some journalists also report gunfire emanating from two ambulances driving towards the headquarters of the Ministry. The government channel advises that there is fighting around the presidential palace in Carthage.'

The staccato rat-tat-tat of gunshots breaks the surreal silence of our neighborhood, confirming the news that we're reading on the web. The strident ringing of our doorbell makes us jump. Who is on the other side of the door?

Curious but ever-cautious, we sneak a peek out the window. It's our immediate neighbor. He's a man with a sharp attitude and an ambiguous sense of humor. He immediately apologizes for scaring us, and asks if we're okay. Then he offers us food and protection, if necessary, concluding with several witticisms about the situation. Bearing in mind that we're foreign, known not to like the cats that live along the road, and remiss about pruning our overgrown bougainvillea – venturing out on our behalf despite the indiscriminate firing of weapons is a very generous and brave gesture, and we're doubly grateful to him.

Like so many other expats, we decide the time has come for us to pack our bags and book seats on the first available flight. The web seems to be down, so we try calling various airlines, but they all shut at 3.00 p.m. and it's now 3.15 pm. We bypass the problem by booking and paying for our flights in Italy with the help of relatives.

They ask us, 'And the return date?' We make a stab and say we'll be back in two weeks, but we hedge our bets by ensuring that the return tickets can be changed. As soon as the deed has been done, we start to wonder whether this departure will be permanent, and whether we, and all the other expats, will ever be allowed to return. We wonder what will happen to our house once we're not here to defend it.

There's a constant flow of communication. News spreads that the presidential palace, a few blocks away from us, is still under attack. Friends living in Tunis post a stream of messages on Facebook, sending text messages, or calling to ensure that we're okay.

The television is showing a constant stream of cartoons, and the kids are glued to it. It gives us an opportunity to pack our bags and prepare more precious things like photographs and valuables that we'll entrust to our landlord and ask him to send to Italy should the situation deteriorate. We finally drop into bed at 1.30 am, but prior to that we reconnect to the internet. It's brimming with reassuring messages from our virtual friends.

'We mustn't panic each time we hear guns being discharged. We need to stay positive. This is a psychological war, and the enemy is terrified, hurting badly and in despair,' comments Monique.

When the night comes, however, it is hard to keep calm among sporadic gunfire and helicopters roaming the sky. Out there in the street, hundreds of people are taking turns blocking the looters and militia. We nevertheless manage to go to sleep.

In the meanwhile in Ghazela, an urban, sprawling neighborhood just outside Tunis, lives Sonia Barbaria, a young Tunisian. She has a much harder time sleeping. She is nine months pregnant. Two days earlier, she joined her husband in the protests at Avenue Bourguiba. 'I am there with my son, as I want him to live in a democracy,' she said to all those questioning her participation. She even had to hide the fact of her attendance from her parents so as not to make them worry. Like many other people, she is glued to her computer, monitoring messages on Facebook and calling friends and relatives to check on them. All of a sudden, her stomach starts hurting – contractions – which pick up and intensify. At 11.00 pm, she writes a post on her Facebook profile 'I think he just decided he wants to be born during curfew, hoping we get to the hospital safe and sound.' Her adventure begins. All the helplines are occupied. There is no way to get someone to escort her. She and her husband rush to their car and head to the hospital with their flashers on, driving at only 30 kilometers per hour. The car gets stopped various times at checkpoints, and the journey seems to last an eternity. At one checkpoint, one army officer loses his temper, fearing that Sonia and her husband are members of some militia. At this point, Sonia is forced to lift her shirt to show her bare pregnant belly.

After three hours, they reach the hospital, still scared. At the hospital, there are few doctors available and no anesthetists. She endures the pain and after one more hour of intense and painful labor, she cries out for joy at still being alive and seeing the arrival of her newborn. She decides to name him Adam, after the first man, according to both the Bible and the Quran. 'He is the first boy to be born in a free Tunisia,' says Sonia.

A BITTER DEPARTURE

*What makes a nation is not speaking the same language or be-
longing to the same ethnographic group, it is having done great
things together in the past and wanting to do more great things
in the future.*

Ernst Renan

January 17ᵗʰ, Carthage/Rome

It's 7.00 am, and we wake up smiling at each other. There's
the staccato of gunfire in the distance.

All set – we are off. We can't, however, drive to the airport in
our old 1994 Fiat 500. The car permit has just expired and nobody thought to go to downtown Tunis to renew it last week.
We turn on our computers to receive the latest updates.

On the roads, the situation is calm. The kiosk round the corner is open, selling what scant goods it has left. The local grocery
store is down to a few oranges and potatoes. Before our departure, we decide to empty our larder and give everything to our
neighbors: couscous, flour, eggs, frozen food, etc. We are leaving, they are staying.

Madam Douja, one of our neighbors, asks us, 'Why are you
leaving? there is nothing to fear.' 'We've decided to return to
our families, to allay their anxieties, just for a little break, but we
will be back,' we reply.

After making its way around a roadblock made up of vases
and even a cactus, the taxi pulls up in front of our house.

We drive through Le Kram, a blue-collar neighborhood next to Carthage, while Karim the taxi driver updates us on the latest news. On the road we see burned-out cars, a tank, soldiers patrolling the streets, and what is left of the little pizzeria. The police station is destroyed, the entry gate wrecked and the columns supporting it have collapsed. It's a long, sad list. The Zitouna Bank[35] has been burnt down, the Orange shop on the opposite side of the road lies destroyed[36]. The Tunisiana[37] shop has had its windows smashed.

We encounter few roadblocks on the way. The airport is packed with people leaving – it resembles a school on the first day of the pupils' return. Some wave to each other; each person will be traveling and carrying with them an unforgettable mix of memories and emotions.

Julia Smith, a friend of ours from the British Embassy, is sitting down near the check-in desks, wearing a fluorescent jacket and holding a small radio. She's coordinating the departure of all the British citizens. She recounts how she spent one night in the embassy's lavatory, as there was nowhere else to sleep. She was in touch with her homologue at the Italian Embassy, who also slept on a chair for eight solid nights. Despite the sleepless night, she carries a great smile and is happy to see us traveling safe.

All airlines, we're informed, have resumed their flights.

---

[35] Zitouna, founded by El Materi, son-in-law of Ben Ali, is the first Islamic Bank of the Maghreb.

[36] The 51% of Orange belonged to Marwan Ben Mabrouk also son-in- law of Ben Ali.

[37] Tunisiana is the name of one of the leading Telecom operator.

After a short flight of little more than an hour we land in our home country, Italy. Upon reaching our family home in Rome, we check the latest developments in Tunis. Suddenly, the air is pierced by the sound of violent explosions. We freeze, exchanging fearful glances.

'You're hearing fireworks!' explains my brother Alessandro. 'Carnival is just around the corner.'

We may be far from Tunis, but we can't stop thinking about it. Even the unexpected bang of a closing shutter makes us jump.

The fear from previous days has morphed into guilt that we've abandoned the revolution when everyone else is doing their utmost to make things return to normal. We think wistfully of our friends left behind.

Monique posts a new message. 'Anyone wishing to do voluntary works at the hospitals please contact me. We need people to change beds, look after the patients, clean, and help personnel.' Within two hours she has received hundreds of messages from people anxious to help. A Tunisian company sends a truck carrying all sorts of food to be donated to all the hospitals.

Lori Severens, one of our friends and neighbors, is still back in Carthage. She decided to stay with her two sons and husband, waiting for things to normalize. After days of staying behind locked doors, she and her husband venture cautiously out in search of food and other supplies. Everyone in the neighborhood is making an effort to help others, offering advice on where to find milk or other staple items, calling down for news from their balconies, and praising the revolution. This open display of neighborliness among strangers is a throwback to the ancient Tunisia, before the oppressive environment and the culture of mutual suspicion instilled by Ben Ali and his regime. The sentiment of pride is new and strong. Lori recounts, 'there is a feeling of hope, of cautious optimism, despite the many unknowns'.

Meanwhile, demonstrations in the city are picking up again, but this time against the temporary government, which seems to contain too many members of the RCD. The population longs to see the end of this party. The 'Movement of the Kasbah' begins with people from all across the country camping in the large esplanade facing the prime minister's office in the homonymous square.

One week later we are back at Rome Airport, checking in for a flight to Tunis. We are going home. The plane is almost empty – there are, perhaps, 15 passengers. Although Tunis is still under curfew, the schools have reopened. Life is returning to normal. For us it's an emotional return to the country to which we feel we belong. We're back in a place where the scent of freedom is as strong as the jasmine in our garden. We feel the overwhelming desire to help build a new nation.

We start writing this book.

Map of Tunisia

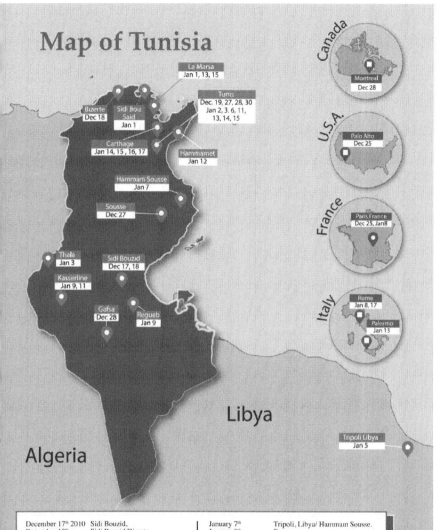

December 17th 2010	Sidi Bouzid,	January 7th	Tripoli, Libya/ Hammam Sousse.
December 18th	Sidi Bouzid/Bizerte.	January 8th	Rome
December 19th	Tunis.	January 9th	Kasserine/Thala/Regueb
December 24th	Rome/London/Menzel Bouzaiene	January 10th	Tunis
December 25th	Paris/California.	January 11th	Tunis/ Kasserine
December 27th	Tunis/Rome	January 12th	Hammamet
December 28th	Tunis/Gafsa/Montreal	January 13rd	Tunis/La Marsa
December 30th	Tunis	January 13rd	Palermo
January 1st, 2011	Sidi Bou Said/ La Marsa.	January 14th.	Carthage/Tunis
January 2nd	Tunis	January 15th	Carthage/ Tunis/ La Marsa
January 4th	Tunis, Ben Arous	January 16th	Carthage
January 6th	Tunis.	January 17th	Carthage/Rome

Made in the USA
Las Vegas, NV
15 January 2022